A BEAUTIFUL DOOM

A collection of poetry and prose
from the heart, soul, and mind of:

Clyde R. Hurlston

copyright © 2024 by Clyde Hurlston. All rights reserved.
Printed in the United States Of America. This book may not be
reproduced or reprinted, unless in the context of reviews,
without prior approval from the author unless otherwise stated.

On behalf of the author, thank you for your purchase.
And may The Hermetic Principles guide us all.

www.clydehurlston.com
facebook.com/adebtpaidinink
@adebtpaidinink

A BEAUTIFUL DOOM

"THE ALLURE OF THE UNKNOWN" ART BY MITCH GREEN

CLYDE HURLSTON

" I'll tell you a secret...
Something they don't teach you in your temple.
The gods envy us.
They envy us, because we're mortal.
Because any moment could be our last.
Everything's more beautiful,
because we're doomed.
You will never be lovelier than you are now.
We will never be here again..."

- Achilles,
(as portrayed by Brad Pitt
in 2004 film, *Troy*.)

I
MEMENTO COGITARE

"Thinking is one thing no one has ever been able to tax."
- Charles Kettering

"No problem can withstand the assault of sustained thinking."
- Voltaire

"Thinking: the talking of the soul with itself."
- Plato

CLYDE HURLSTON

"CONTEMPLATION" ART BY MITCH GREEN

COLLECTIVE MISERY

I had so many things I wanted to say,
but I can't find the words anymore.
So many projects were started,
but I lack the desire to see them through.
I'm sure a handful of you will ask why,
but the reasons aren't important.
All you need to know
is that the ideas overwhelm me,
and the only things that get executed
are my hopes. So rather than let them
bleed out slowly, I may as well
put them out of their collective misery.
Because that is all they ever seem
to bring me... Misery.
But I'm not going to spend
anymore time bitching about it.
Some fates must be accepted.
So this is me signing off for awhile.
I wish you all the best.
May your days be wonderful.

HUBRIS

The sun will bring
the promise of tomorrow;
But the moon shines
on the darkness of night.
Adrenaline is a teacher,
Preparing us for battle or flight.
I won't contribute to the suffering
Nor will I ever know
the embrace of the sky.
Since I'm far too busy falling,
For ones who'll never know I'm alive.
So enjoy the view of Daedalus,
As I plunge headfirst in the sea.
For some of us deserve to remember,
How steep the price of hubris can be…

THE TRUTH ABOUT ANGELS

It has taken me
many, many years
to learn the truth
about the way this game
was to be played.
It took much trial and error;
and it caused much pain.
Along with more than enough heartbreak.
But in the end,
I believe the knowledge
was worth the cost.
For I've learned that nature
will always favor the moon;
while time will always favor the sun.
And I have learned that angels,
will often resent being treated,
as if they are a sinner's saving grace.
Instead preferring to trade
their halos for horns,
if they are publicly granted
the winner's chosen place.

CLYDE HURLSTON

THE COST OF BEING WRONG

Today, I realized that
I have been a fool.
I've placed my
unrealistic expectations
on both greedy and
beautiful souls alike.
And for that, I beg all of you,
to accept this inscribed,
yet overdue apology.
I've learned that it was wrong of me
to expect anything from people
other than what they
had already given me.
My hopes were never
their burden to bear;
nor was blood ever
supposed to come from stones.
For even if Prometheus
stole fire on my behalf,
it was still wrong
of me to expect warmth.
I understand that now.
So for those who continue to give,
you will forever receive
my earnest gratitude.
But for the rest of my days,
I fear I must be sparing with my hopes,
and economical with my dreams.
For I've reached a point in life,
where my mind cannot afford
the cost of my heart being wrong.

REFLECTIONS OF JANUS

How could I have been so blind?
Falling prey to both
my hubris and stubbornness,
I ignored the Reflections Of Janus.
Ever was I the myopic fool;
so inured by the past,
that I've allowed it to craft my present
on the precipice of the future.
Ignoring the most basic of the principles:
as above, so below.
These celestial alignments
are never by chance.
I must let go, in order to be received.
I must summon the valor
to journey and gaze in
the reflecting pools of my dreams.
One of blue, one of green.
Showing me the places I can go,
and the places that I've been.
I wonder if she will have me.
Shall I be welcomed into her temple,
now that I have been
weighed and found wanting?
Oh, how I wish it to be.
May she read these words and know,
that though I may nervously
stumble into her garden,
I am truly prepared to grow.

CLYDE HURLSTON

THE EXPANSE

Picking myself up off the ground,
my mind beheld a ladder
with only five rungs.
It was leaning against an oak tree,
which possessed branches that reached
as far as the eye could see.
And I wondered to myself,
if the darkness I was feeling
could actually be shade.
But as it turned out, on this day,
there was no illumination to be had.
Perspective sometimes comes only,
when it's stumbling drunk and uninvited.
So there must come a time,
when you must pick up the pieces,
and make the mosaics on your own.
For the bigger picture has been said to lie,
just beyond the scope
of your frame of mind.
The truth lies in the expanse;
and it is waiting for those
with the courage to seek it.
But never rely solely on a guide;
for their journey is theirs,
and your conclusions
may be tainted by their lens.

A REVOLVING DOOR

A revolver slowly raised,
has been said to paint a pretty picture.
But I'd rather place
the gunpowder in these lines,
that I'll fashion into scripture.
Understanding is the bullet,
that's been chambered with intent.
Yet they've placed the safety on our souls,
so the salvo's never sent.
For in the hands of any master,
all things become a weapon.
Leaving the truth to be sequestered,
as care is killed beyond the septum.
Was our collective conscience
frozen by design?
Or merely lacking solar heat?
With the blade and chalice separated,
was their Phyrric victory our defeat?
I believe the answer's yes,
but it wasn't chiseled into stone.
So I must remove my shackles,
before I can help you remove your own.
Our wills can then combine,
and maybe turn this ship around.
Before the darkened ones behind the veil,
drive us straight into the ground.

CLYDE HURLSTON

ENGINEERED THE FALL

There has been a shift in understanding,
but it hasn't come with age.
I haven't lost myself in holy books,
nor devoured every page.
I've merely opened up my mind,
as others spoke the truth.
Comparing it to every single word,
I was exposed to in my youth.
As if it were engineered,
we were children led astray.
While given new technologies,
to keep our growing souls at play.
For the profane were not allowed,
to ever glance beyond the veil.
Nor did we learn the reasons why,
She was blind and held the scales.
Oh, they hid the stars inside their lines,
knowing that the Seven ruled us all.
Like demons, they hoarded
every trace of Grace,
so how could we do anything but fall?

THY WILL BE DONE

How is it possible?
For seeds to have been
sown throughout the ages?
Seemingly out of sight,
but never out of mind.
And as the precessions moved us
through the houses, what was planted
blossomed inside the subconscious.
Then watered by the ego,
it was writ large into existence.
But how can we encompass
the entirety of all into three letters?
How could we have known that
this practice existed
long before the masses
were fed with fish and loaves?
It's simple, my friend;
we were never supposed to know.
Our unwashed hands were never meant
to part the veil;
and our journeys were meant
to remain completely "unbegun."
But some of us are awakening;
and we have every intention
of sowing seeds of our own.
Only this time, the original three demand
it be done beneath the Sun.

CLYDE HURLSTON

THE MANY FORMS OF MARTYRDOM

Martyrdom comes in many forms, my friend.
Whether you are forcing a soul
to pay for the sins of another,
or you are willing to sacrifice yourself
for a cause you feel to be just;
there is a martyr in all of us.
And lately I've come to find that for me,
the definition has changed.
I find myself living to help those
who don't even know I am alive.
I lose myself beneath the weight
of my own expectations.
And I often destroy myself by loving people
who will never feel the same way.
Yes my friend, it seems that
even here in the tower,
the nails still find their way into my wrists.
And the blood still makes love to the floor.
So once the curtain closes
on my self-imposed insanity,
I hope the gods are merciful.

THE PITY PARADE

Tell me, baby... what is the point
of this constant game you play?
This popping in and out of people's lives,
as if you've grown allergic to stability.
Knowing full well that without
your prescription for attention filled,
you'll become the Grand Marshall
of your very own pity parade.
And those of us foolish enough to care,
will wave our hands next to the float,
hoping to catch one
of your hand-crafted stories.
You know, those worthless things
that are often rife with contradictions,
and held together by excuses.
Look around, beautiful.
See how we marvel at the carnival;
for your cavalcade
of self-inflicted tragedies is endless.
And while there are some
who may be eager
to shower you in sympathy,
I'm starting to realize
I haven't had this much fun in years.
So come on, cry me something, darling...

CLYDE HURLSTON

THE BURDEN OF IDEAS

Because of the burden
of consciousness,
sometimes we overcompensate.
Some people drink,
some people smoke,
some people snort...
some people fuck.
Others they crave isolation.
But all of us find ourselves
overwhelmed with ideas.
These thoughts... of who we are,
who we were,
or who we're supposed to be.
But here I am... overwhelmed again.
Fighting back the tears,
and realizing that I'm not
who I thought I was.
Afraid that I'll never become
who I want to be.
All the while, I'm just stumbling
in the fucking dark.
But I swear,
I just want to do the right thing.

THE BELOVED STONE

With intentions instead of shovels,
I dug a hole deep within my chest.
As if driven mad with these compulsions,
my soul lying heavy from unrest.
And with the strength of Atlas,
I opened ribs in the guise of vise.
Knowing actions demand a sacrifice,
was ready and willing to pay the price.
I quickly threw my hands into the mire,
searching for a trace of gold.
As I bathed myself in royal blood,
I found the answer seldom told.
For these true journeys of discovery,
must be embarked upon alone.
Then you'll discover
alchemy's beloved stone,
is the beating heart you call your own.

CLYDE HURLSTON

WITH HEARTS IN HAND

I've lost count of the number of times
I've drowned on dry land.
Forced to watch the things
I've wanted most in life,
pull away from me
and leave me to the elements.
Each time becoming another reminder
that life is merciless
to those with hearts in hand.
That is why I've chosen to remain
here within the bell tower.
For here my manual labor provides
some semblance of purpose,
and this wretched visage
will harm the eyes of no one.
Lepers belong out of reach.
And when you abstain from love and lust,
I find there's less bleeding to be done.
If only I had learned this sooner...

WHEN THE RED BEGINS TO RUN

For all of her brilliance,
she might as well have been dumb.
For all of her tenacity,
she might as well have been timid.
For all of her strength,
she might as well have been brittle.
For all of her vigor,
she might as well have been dead.
For all of her love,
she might as well have succumb to hate.
Because her scars
have become watermarks;
showing those who pay attention,
just how high the tears would rise.
Knowing full well that martyrdom
wasn't her intention,
she still blames herself on a daily basis.
Unable to help but wonder aloud,
"How could a man possess such a gravity,
that she could lose herself within?
How could the blacks of his eyes
breed stars, causing her
to get close enough to count?
How could she venture
beyond his event horizon,
and still hope to make a home?
How could she have her mind blown
when she was on her back,
and then stand, only to be told
of all the things she lacks?"
What is she to do,
when everything she's given,
clearly isn't enough?
Oh Lord, when her red begins to run,
how could she be anything but done?

CLYDE HURLSTON

ALL THAT'S LEFT IS RIGHT

At night, I find myself
picking at memories as if they were scabs.
Poking and prodding at them,
until I can get a fingernail
underneath the edge and lift.
Letting the blood flow just a little bit.
Exposing a scar that was already there.
This foolish errand all done
in a lonely man's crude attempts to feel again.
Hoping the scents and sounds
will come flooding back,
and help him to ignore the silence
booming loudly in his room.
Praying that an empty bed
will eventually begin to feel like her skin.
All the while,
knowing good and goddamn well
that once my ink dries, so will her interest.
For my poetic prophecies
have always come true!
Yet instead of being able to smile
and recall the many times she said "I love you."
I instead shudder and remind myself
of my accuracy by
constantly saying, "I told you so."
Fuck, man...
I wonder if Nostradamus
ever grew tired of being right.
Because I know I certainly have.

HERALD

I am the collective fate
of a thousand whispers.
I am the blurred line
between expectation
and disappointment.
I am the place where happiness
hides its splendor,
and despair unearths bravado.
I am the proof that
passion belies its age,
When falling short of promise.
I am the merciless, southern sun
upon untreated skin.
I am the fading throes of a love
once given to misinterpreted royalty.
And I am the
regretful knees once bent
in honor of echoed,
unanswered prayers.
I am everything.
I am nothing.
To everyone. To no one.
Herald of words.
Proven unworthy of love.
Unworthy of breath.

CLYDE HURLSTON

BEFORE IT'S TOO LATE

The Deciders are at it again.
Making decisions in private
that will alter the course
of the future for the public.
For decades now,
they have continued
feeding that malignant
Creature From Jekyll Island.
And now, they want to give it full control.
But this time,
it is the preservation of the planet
that will act as the velvet glove
hiding their iron fist.
While we sit and argue
amongst ourselves
about the color of our parties,
the color of our collars,
and even the color of our skin...
they are planning their Great Reset.
Gone are the days when
they hid only in Groves
or lofty boardrooms.
No, they do these things
out in the open now.
Giving each subversive group and policy
these lovely and benign names;
lulling us into further apathy
and a less-than-passive interest.
And because there is
nothing new under the sun,
if one is looking, you can easily see
their open hands reaching
for the levers of old.
Thankfully, so many of us
are beginning to wake now.
Especially since their mandates for masks

have caused their own to slip.
We are able to see the ones
who are using our concerns
as Trojan horses, with which
they will trample that Lady
standing in the harbor.
My friends, we must stand with her.
Before it is too late.
Otherwise, the greatest idea
in the history of creation,
will be lost to time.

CLYDE HURLSTON

EROSION

My heart is much like
my beloved Louisiana landscape.
Slowly washing away.
Eroded by the passage of time
and abuse from the waves.
And despite the bit of sun today,
it is has rained for awhile here.
Rained with anger and a bitter discontent.
And now the bayous and canals are full
and the water has no place else to go.
So it comes pouring onto the streets,
the ones that run forever
like the veins inside my arms.
And while flooding is a common occurrence,
there are still some, poor souls
who are never prepared for it.
Even though, deep down they know,
they've brought it upon themselves.
The water comes creeping in
beneath the doors,
and they scream in shock.
Flailing about like injured wildlife.
It's such a pathetic sight.
At least the animals know better.
They left for higher ground weeks ago.
But not the fool.
No, the fools drown before they know
that it's time to swim.
And in their last few seconds,
their eyes well up, as they wonder
why no one came from the skies
to build them an ark.

PENLIGHTS

Like many others,
I too often fall prey to my own thoughts.
As I make my way throughout each day,
all it takes is a minor setback
or some unexpected occurrence,
and my mind runs away with me.
Almost as if those few seconds
prove to be cracks in a dam
no one else can see;
the only thing that stands
between the outside world and
my ocean of emotions.
And as I sit there trying to restrain myself,
I focus on my breathing;
hoping that each deep breath
becomes another hand
over each growing geyser in the wall.
Thankfully, I am able to remind myself
that today wasn't as bad
as I thought it would be.
Staving off the seemingly,
inevitable collapse. How?
Because I was able to remember
that I am alive and
I am blessed to be healthy;
despite this clearly, imperfect frame.
And some days, that has to be enough.
Even if I didn't accomplish
all of my goals for the day,
I still made it through the day.
And that counts for something.
So if you are out there reading this,
please know that no matter
what the voice in your head may tell you,
the sun will rise in the morning.
And when the hours

CLYDE HURLSTON

feel like crosses to bear,
just try your hardest
to find some joy within the minutes.
Because when we're not looking,
roses can grow between the fingers
of the second hand.
We just have to remind ourselves
to stop and smell them.
So on days when
your moon is not in sight,
and dawn feels too far away...
I pray you will allow
these words to find you.
Like they were penlights in the darkness.

AD ASTRA

When one begins
reaching toward the stars,
They begin reaching toward you.
It is then that
one must forego the self,
And beat back
the beast with stillness.
For it is only when
the serpent ascends,
finally reaching the crown,
that one then discovers "God."

CLYDE HURLSTON

WHERE DO WILTING ROSES GO?

I watch as some roses shirk the sun,
Fearing what its light reveals.
They'll claim preference for the shade,
While forsaking shadow work that heals.
Still, I can't help but wonder why
Some cycles will oft repeat
Before she finally wises up
And keeps solid ground beneath her feet.
For it's in this beholder's eyes
She left other flowers with no room
But now I'm here and asking where
Do all the wilting roses go
After they've had their chance to bloom?

SOFTLY NESTING

At night, I lie awake;
my soul stirred by noises
that were never made aloud.
Upon a closer look,
I find you there. As always.
Softly nesting in my memories.
Knowing that for me,
this is the only proof of
your existence these days.
For these eyes have seen your face
less than they have seen miracles.
And that is fine.
You have your reasons, after all.
In truth, find myself
caring less these days.
About myself. About humanity.
About existence.
All I hold dear tonight, is this empty bed.
At least here I know that I was missed.
For my place was held
as if I had never left.
Same as the one you shunned
so many moons ago.
Yet we take comfort
where we find it, I guess.
Yours was down a path
you felt you never should've took.
And mine resides in a place,
I just no longer care to look.

CLYDE HURLSTON

LOOK AWAY

On a rain-soaked night,
I found myself alone and unable to sleep.
After tossing and turning for awhile,
the ceiling became the work of art
on which I fixated.
When suddenly a voice
inside my head thought,
"You've been abandoned by your sun,
and forsaken by your moon,
so who could blame you
for wanting to look away."
But I've grown tired
of listening to the darkness.
So I got up and decided
to take a walk outside.
And as the rain fell down upon me,
helping me to hide
the tears within my eyes,
I found the strength to whisper
a quiet prayer to myself:
"Don't look away...
You must instead
find the courage to look up.
For even though the night is dark,
your stars are still there.
Even when you can't see them."

CHARM THE SERPENT

Is all but lost when one seeks outwardly?
Is there nothing but antiquated customs
and barbaric texts with which
to find oneself?
Is all we know the way
that Mani once perceived it to be?
My friend, I do not know for certain.
But I have felt the crushing loneliness
that comes with stumbling
out of Plato's cave.
Like proverbial trees, I have fallen
and made no sound
as I sought to overturn every stone.
But a wise man once told me
that I too must wrestle the angel.
Only then I can charm
the coiled serpent to rise,
and take me to the place
where Jacob met God face to face.
Though I fear I am not close enough
to reach the summit just yet;
with the words of the masters
and with The Seven guiding my steps,
I can proudly say that I am on the way.

CLYDE HURLSTON

LOSE YOURSELF

Wade into the wonders of my words.
Lose yourself inside a love
that coats like ink, but tastes like wine.
A place where you will lose
all sense of direction,
along with your very sense of time.
Do not be fooled by
the calmness of the waves, darling.
For it is when the reservoir is most still,
that the waters run the deepest.
And it's where a demi-goddess
once bragged about
how well she could swim;
only to claim she was in over her head,
so she needed to return home.
It is the place where
a Queen found refuge
for what I hoped to be forever.
But after she rejuvenated herself,
she found her strength to swim
to the shores of another.
Such is life, I'm afraid.
Still I bid you again
to place yourself inside these lines.
I know that you will never stay;
you will just stare
at your reflection for a time.
And then I'll be washed away in your eyes
like all sand castles should be.
But I promise, neither of us
will be the same afterwards.

THE ONE THAT BLEEDS

Look at you now.
Like the fabled fool at the reflecting pool...
No! Do not avert thy gaze, Creator.
Affix thine eyes upon this
ungodly monster you have made.
For it is your cavalcade of mistakes
that I have borne
like crosses upon the hill.
It is your doubts that eat away
at the back of my eyes when given silence.
And it is your inaction
that has buried me beneath
this most wretched visage.
How dare you forsake that
which you took a lifetime to make!
What gives you the right?!
Who gave you the authority
to drive nails inside my wrists
and then masquerade as if
you were the thief crucified beside me?
Well I do not forgive you!
For you know exactly what you do!
And after all this time,
who allowed you to defile
the one thing that gave
my once pathetic existence meaning?
And who made you the whore
of both sinner and saint alike?
You did, Creator.
You and your naivety.
You and your stupid heart.
By the gods, I curse it.
Along with this stupid tower.
For it is often your heart that beats,
but I am always the one that bleeds.

CLYDE HURLSTON

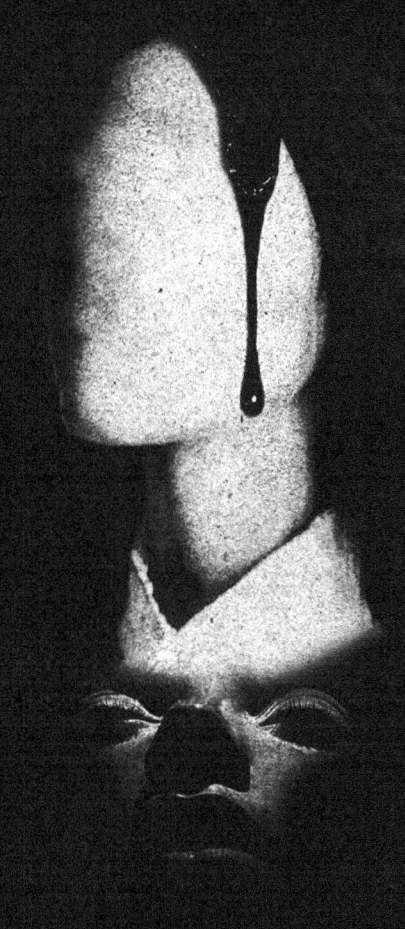

"THE BLEEDING" ART BY MITCH GREEN

THE WAR FOR HEAVEN

Like the ancients,
I found her divine influence everywhere.
If consulted, I would say
that I believed it to was the chance
of watching her wake,
that gave the sun the confidence to shine.
If I were placed upon the stand,
I would swear, it was the way she said
"good morning, baby"
that put the rapid movement in the trees.
And if pressed I would confess,
that I imagined it was merely the thought
of touching her, that brought the tides
home upon the shore.
Yet, after all this time,
I have been far removed from her grace.
Gone are the days
when she blazed across my skies;
making mine eyes both witnesses to glory
and the envy of the worlds.
But now she bathes herself in silence,
and travels long distances
to dry her perfect face.
Oh god, I've realized that
my mind and my heart
are still at war over their heaven;
tell me, can the forsaken
ever regain their favor in her eyes?

CLYDE HURLSTON

UNWANTED PIECES

Others have spilled their blood
upon these pages,
and have been revered for it.
Others have encapsulated
the imagination of the masses,
using merely a few words or lines.
And then there is me...
Trying to find the clarity
of mirrors within their pieces.
Producing a cavalcade of shards
that seem to do nothing
but harm the souls
that once sought to handle them.
I promise this was never my intention,
but it happens all the same.
Not that it matters,
I doubt they will have to
put up with me for much longer.

BENEATH THE STRATA

I have once again failed
to take heed of the sands
falling within the glass.
And in my zeal to proceed
without deception, I've unearthed
truths that are far better
left buried beneath the strata.
That is when the silence
descends upon us like the plague.
Words once uttered hang in the air
for a sliver of eternity,
becoming burdens to lips
now filled with regret.
Yet through the thick haze of confusion,
assurances are made profusely;
though they bring not even
a modicum of comfort.
For the lepers know
they do not belong
in the public squares;
and forsaking the safety
of their shadows,
will always have
the gravest of consequences.
So do not fret if this tongue falls quiet.
I am merely retaking
the place that I deserve.

CLYDE HURLSTON

BURN WITH LIFE

Deception is pervasive in the world...
I can see that plainly
from here within the tower.
Yet, I begrudgingly come down
from time to time and
lose myself amongst the buzzing crowds.
Because despite our collective distrust,
one must always continue
to breathe life into our humanity.
For isolation often leads to apathy.
And without moderation,
solitude can become the chalice
from which the nihilist drinks;
so I refuse to allow myself
to go to that place again.
That place where all is dark
and not even the gods
can find an ember to fuel their existence.
Make no mistake though, dear friend.
I shall remain vigilant.
For there are souls in my life
worth dying to protect,
and it is in their name
and my own that I shall
continue to burn with life.
Sovereignty nears when
these truths are known.
Mark my words.

UNDESERVED WOUNDS

These eyes have watched
some dreams wither upon the vine,
and they've seen some
go through metamorphosis with time.
Some are birthed and grow,
to become the dreamer's status quo.
While some die their quiet deaths,
and venture to the place where dreams
were never carried on our breaths.
And such is life...
Today, I can taste the hint of salt
as the tears choose my face
to be their final resting place;
because I learned my dream died today.
And I don't even care enough to bury it.
I'd rather leave it rotting in the sun,
as a reminder to the rest,
of the romantic fools,
there are consequences to
the rose-colored glasses that we use.
It makes it harder to see the blood,
when we're dying from both
undeserved wounds
and completely broken hearts.

CLYDE HURLSTON

AN OCEAN OF WAVES

Today, for the first time in my life,
I felt myself take pity upon the ocean.
Why? You may ask...
It's because even with all of its beauty
and all of its power,
I have watched in silent horror
as its splendor was all but distilled
to the mere passing of a wave.
And though each wave
proclaims themselves to be far
different from the next,
they are truly one and the same.
Still they all know the truth, deep down.
Because they continuously rise and fall
against the most enticing stones
lying on the shores that catch their eyes.
Is it no surprise then,
that they crash frequently;
only to be left broken,
once the excitement recedes?
Becoming a fraction
of what they were previously.
Sure, they always find a way
to come back together;
but by that time, their precious depths
have gone unexplored.
The interest of their chosen shore
is all but eroded, having been taken
by the passing of another wave.
And so the story goes.
On and on, throughout eternity.
I wonder if the gods laugh
at such foolish tragedies;
or do they consider us all
the stars of their divine comedy?

IRONY

Why is it that
when I want to write,
the words they never come?
Yet, when I think about the person
I've been dying to forget,
the words they never stop?
Life is but a cruel irony.

CLYDE HURLSTON

THE OCEAN AT NIGHT

I've since come to realize that
I'm not the picture of perfection;
instead I am the ocean late at night.
Not made to be enjoyed by anyone,
but rather remaining in motion
just beyond your line of sight.
When enraged,
the waves come with force,
destroying anything on land.
When at rest,
the depths are oft profound,
leaving few who understand.
And I'm sure if you could ask her,
she'd tell you of my warmth,
even on the coldest days.
And she'd say that I was humble,
never behaving in the boldest ways.
She loved me for
the heart that I displayed,
said it was something
the world had never seen.
And so she crowned me as her King,
while living beside me as a Queen.
But now circumstances
have provided change,
so the roles have been recast.
And I find myself boiling
beneath the surface,
when thinking about my past.
I find it hard to move forward,
when I got accustomed
to living out a dream.
Now I simply thrash about in darkness,
using each written wave
as the expression of a scream.
For I still miss her everyday.

LAST RESORT

A heart was poured out
and then it dried.
Leaving eyes to see
after they had cried.
That all he gave,
he gave in vain.
And they never see you bleed,
when they don't understand your pain.
So pick up the pieces,
you're on your own.
This is not the first time
that you've been alone.
Hell, it's anything else
that would be the shock.
You were bred to live between
both the hard place and the rock.
So let those who've lied to you
see just what you'll become.
As they wonder where
your new attitude is coming from.
But they'll fail to see
that it was always there.
You keep it as a last resort,
for when you no longer care.
From here on out,
it's good riddance to them all.

CLYDE HURLSTON

FLOWERS IN THE ATTIC

In me, she saw potential,
and said there was
a king beneath the dust.
But my warning signs were posted,
and they revealed my broken trust.
Yet still she walked toward me,
since a challenge suits her best.
And like a moth, kept drawing closer to,
what beats within my chest.
She said it's a heart the size of Texas,
and you can often hear it roar.
But it seems there have been
too many times,
that its pieces were left upon the floor.
Still she couldn't help but wonder,
just what hid behind my eyes.
Are there treasures to be found within,
or is there only emptiness and lies?
So her words would help me open,
the attic sealed for years.
She made her way through dying vines,
that some would call my fears.
And her touch became the water,
that would help the flowers grow.
If only she had stayed awhile,
who knows what other wonders
I could've learned to show...

THE CURRENCY OF THE GODS

When I look around,
all I see are horrors.
The devastation in life
coming painfully close
to suffocating the beauty.
The world has become a place
where greed has overrun
the house of love;
yet no one seems to care anymore.
So many souls live
in a perpetual motion,
yet their flames lie extinguished.
They exist as smoldering ruins
amidst a larger tapestry of decay.
And so, I'm forced to think,
"By the gods, who stole their wonder?
Where, in all the worlds,
has their imagination gone?"
I know it is missing,
because I too was like them.
So engulfed in hubris,
and so angry from betrayals,
that I once denied the unknowable.
Choking on four-letter words
bathed in cynicism, I raged.
Assuming every shepherd
led to a slaughterhouse.
But now I know,
the hourglass is not a prison;
and its sands hide not the guillotine.
The length of eternity
cannot be measured by a ruler.
That which may be seen
is tempted by the scale;
that which may only be felt,
is akin to gravity.
That is the power of The Creator
and the currency of the gods.
Who are you to say otherwise?

CLYDE HURLSTON

THE PACKAGE

Someday...
That is what they tell themselves.
Someday, that in which they seek,
shall find them. It shall find them
and love them with an intensity
that will make their wait worthwhile.
I hear such things,
and truthfully, I laugh.
For I know it is but a hollow promise;
a promise made by the heart
seeking forgiveness from the mind
for the pains of past decisions.
And in an attempt to
prove themselves worthy,
they languish in a self-imposed exile;
claiming to be on a journey
to find that which was never truly lost.
That which was simply disregarded
in a cloud of love, lust,
and dreams of tomorrows never lived.
My, what fools they are.
Blind to the ends of their noses
and the proximity of their desires;
yet it's the package that
makes it so easy to miss.
The package that inspires
revulsion or indifference;
and most likely, never devotion.
Such truths are painful things;
and I fear in some cases,
much deserved.

A PRAYER FROM THE UNCHOSEN

Examine every angle, darling.
Remove yourself from the maelstrom,
and give yourself
the greatest vantage point.
Look not with the heart, nor the eyes...
Rather seek only with the mind.
For what beats only feels
and will cloud one's judgment.
What blinks only interprets
and can be misled by illusions.
Yet, what thinks only falls prey to time.
Until then, it ventures from the past,
into the present,
and even into the future.
So be wary, love.
May reason always guide your rhyme,
and may logic always find you,
until the end of your time.
I wish you nothing else.

CLYDE HURLSTON

THE HOURGLASS OF ETERNITY

These are strange times
we're living in, my friend.
The hallmarks of wanton violence
and obsessive avarice
litter the ever-changing landscape.
Most of us see through
the eyes of the cynic,
and no longer have the strength
to change this world;
because we are far too busy
trying to keep our heads above water.
Drowning in our respective debts
and our own personal hells.
We look to the gods
for meaning in this existence;
so that we may pretend our lives
are something more than
exquisite sand castles,
being slowly eroded by the tides of time.
Our days but grains of sand
in the hourglass of eternity.
Yes, we endure all of this,
knowing that most of us have nothing
but regrets and memories to keep us warm.
But I believe it's high time
we took those pieces of ourselves
and fashioned them into crowns;
for there are no masters but us.
And it's when we realize our sovereignty,
that the stars will look down
upon us with reverence;
and all that is below
will mirror all that is above.

A DEEP-SEATED LONGING

I once heard a man say
that time is a flat circle;
and that all we have ever done,
we are destined to do again.
If that is the case, how does one explain
the monarch butterfly?
Toward the end of every year,
their population begins
their southern migration;
hoping to escape the harshness of winter
and journey into
the warmer parts of Mexico.
Yet no single butterfly
completes the entire trip.
Four generations complete the annual cycle.
So how do the growing butterflies
know where to go?
How does one know to continue
a journey they never started,
and long for a place they've never been?
This leaves me thinking
of my very first breaths.
As Alan Watts once said,
as I woke up despite
never having been asleep.
Now I'm left to wonder,
are we butterflies in our own ways?
Are we sovereigns on our own journeys,
tracing the paths of our ancestors?
For some of us,
it would certainly appear so.
How else could we have come
so close to the sun,
without ever having left the ground?

CLYDE HURLSTON

MY LAST ASCENSION

Be still your body,
and carry your mind
to the farthest reaches of space,
and know that I am there.
Stand proudly, and fix your eyes
downward into the very dirt
beneath your feet,
and know that I am there as well.
Place your hand upon your chest,
feel your heart
as it mirrors the drums of war;
proving that you are indeed alive.
And in the silence between each beat,
do you know what you'll discover?
That I am there.
You may ask yourself
how I could make such a claim;
do I believe myself to be a god?
Yet the truth is
so very far from that, my friend.
I am not divine;
the spark that lit the fuse
of my existence, was.
For I am the imperfect result
of perfected creation.
I am the collapsing star
that seared flesh
onto the bones of this avatar.
I am the monad given sentience,
the lower reflection
of the archangels above.
I am the stumbling child,
relearning all that I've forgotten
since my last ascension.
And most importantly,
of all the things that I am... I am here.
So that means there is
plenty of work to be done.
Will you help me help us all?

LE ROI EST MORT...

Not many people know
that I was once a king.
They're even more shocked to learn
that I ruled on two separate occasions.
The first time my reign
lasted only for a night,
in the small town of LaPlace.
The second time, I reigned in secret;
and the details needn't be spoken
to those uninitiated to my work.
But as I lie in this empty bed tonight,
I have rediscovered a truth that
has helped to keep the melancholy at bay.
My past reigns did not end
because I was unworthy;
rather, they ended because
there must be seasons
to things of such intensity.
For no man is free
from the principle of rhythm;
the universe decrees it!
So it is with that in mind
that I submit to the truth,
and aim to put the past to bed.
"The king is dead, long live the King!"
as they so often say.
But they should know
my ascension begins today...
I will reign again!
Then, and only then,
shall my Queen find me.
I believe this shall come to pass.

CLYDE HURLSTON

THE STRANGER

Reflected off the glass, I saw a person
who was clearly a stranger to me.
His eyes were kind, yet full of sorrow.
As if he was disappointed in
the state he found me in.
But without hesitation he spoke to me,
and what he said stopped me in my tracks.
He said, "You mustn't allow yourself
to get discouraged.
Because you will come to learn
that great changes happen over time.
A river doesn't create canyons over night;
yet, it eventually gets where
it was supposed to be.
Your journey is exactly the same.
Promise me you won't allow
the darkness to get the best of you!
Know that the way out is forward,
and the way up is within.
Remember these things that I've said!
One day you will understand!"
And as I continued fighting
the embrace of sleep,
I sat up and rubbed my eyes.
And as I was cleaning these
windows to my soul, I wondered
if the stranger in the mirror was right...
Am I making my way toward the light?

THE WELL OF LIFE

Fear not my friend,
for I too have often wondered
about my purpose in life.
I've always believed it was
sharing my thoughts with first the page,
and then with the world;
by proxy calling myself
a writer or even a poet.
Yet as I go back and read
the words of the masters,
I dare not count myself amongst them.
I'm not in that league.
I'm just a man seeking to making sense
of my own thoughts and the world I live in.
So it's then I wonder,
who am I without this pen in my hand?
Who could I be when I'm not
suffering beneath depression's kiss?
Is there not more within the well of life,
from which I may pull?
Friend, I believe there is.
And on days like today,
the sun feels like a glowing crown
that I may one day earn upon my head.
For it knows that I don't want to be
better than anyone;
except the man I was yesterday.
And I want to rule nothing
but my own thoughts and actions.
The principle of mentalism
has shown me this is possible;
I must simply act to make it so.
I hope you will continue with me
on this journey,
knowing that you can do the same.

CLYDE HURLSTON

REBELLION

For some of us,
rebellion is not an act;
nor is it a trend.
It is a habit.
A reflexive action.
One consciously committed,
when going against the grain
is the only way to go.
And having said that,
may Heaven help,
those who would stand in our way
of doing what is right.

EDEN'S OUT OF REACH

O, holder of ancient wisdom
Come unto me I beg
Come and fill mine empty hands
And still each painfully, unsteady leg
Deliver unto this wretch
Both your certainty and truth
Bestow the gifts that come with age
And not the ignorance of youth
For these are times I cannot bear
And there are days I no longer wish to live
Still it is the remaining parts of me
That I am expected now to give
But what can be said for we the foolish
Masquerading as the brave
Knowing that the closest we'll get to Eden
Is lying on our backs within a grave.

CLYDE HURLSTON

SUBCONSCIOUS MAGNETS

I know that the temptations surround us all.
Throughout every second of every day,
a cavalcade of information
now lies a fingertip away.
And I must admit I feel the pull;
as if the metaphoric hooks
have latched onto my very soul.
I see all of these so-called miracles,
eagerly sold to the callers willing to act now.
Whether it is a pill to help me lose all
of these unwanted pounds without exercise,
or the wisdom from some guru who
will help me become a god in the bedroom.
Maybe it is someone who will teach me how
to dress and be noticed by women,
or it could be the latest get-rich-quick scheme
or even another beauty product
with some celebrity's name on it...
All of these things are like
aphrodisiacs to the lost.
Subconscious magnets pulling
at the weaknesses behind our eyes.
Each possessing appeal to a man
who has always felt like less than.
But I know the truth; our situations cannot
be changed without hard, grueling work.
As for whether it needs to be done
in the light or in the Shadows,
well that depends on the soul.

HER WORDS, NOT MINE (PART 2)

She said, "I've always loved your visits,
And I wish they never had to end.
Since each is better than the one before
It is the most amazing trend.
But this life, it takes us many ways
Yet we always work to reunite
And give each other such rewards
It makes the waiting a delight
But I must confess, there is a stress
When the urge threatens to consume
And lonely hands are not enough
So I need you here inside my room
And though I always pay the price
On days that follow up our nights
It's a cost I pay without regret
For pain mixed with pleasure is a vice
And while many settle for fantasies
Using toys or trashy novels to pretend
I don't have to do a single thing
Since I can still feel exactly where you've been
And if I were to stand or cross my legs
The results would be quite severe
But don't mistake me for a second, love
I only came because you were here
And with each of the throbbing pains
I feel inside me when I move
More than memories start flooding back
When I recall the point you had to prove
But I've said that you're my best so many times
By now it should be branded in your head
For we both know that not a man compares
To the way you take care of me in bed
And I say such things with honesty
Because they're exactly how I feel
And our dynamic's best described as rare
That's why its power is so real
So I'll do my best to give you breathing room

CLYDE HURLSTON

Throughout the days we live to see
But you better not give it to another soul
The same way you give your love to me.
Because every inch of it is mine."
And dear friends, I couldn't help but smile
As I read her typed confession on my phone.
Knowing this was yet another poetic case
Of these being her words, and not my own.

WILL I EVER LEARN?

Stars will shine,
above monuments aligned.
But for the life of me,
I just can't seem to escape
the gravity of past decisions.
Will I ever learn to let go?

CLYDE HURLSTON

GRACED WITH SHADE

Why do we pray for rain?
When it just makes mud of the dirt.
And there's no escaping pain.
Are we better off embracing the hurt?
For at best we're graced with shade.
Since it's so hard to hide from the sun.
May gathered parts provide a sum.
Before all in the day is said and done.

THE DIFFERENCE BETWEEN TASTE & TRUTH

It never ceases to amaze me
how fast things can change.
In this time I've been exiled,
I have often wondered
if light envied the speed
in which blessings once prayed for
can eventually become considered burdens.
After all, aren't the perceptions
of the eyes as fluid as the tears
that sometimes fall from them?
I ask this because
despite being able to recall
with clarity the few times
I have had a place within the apple,
I've found myself on the wrong side
of the eyes more often than not.
And with so many options to choose from,
is it any wonder that
with just a few fallen grains,
shade can be treated as shadow?
Just as idiosyncrasies once cherished
can suddenly be interpreted
as unforgivable indignations.
All because we live in a world
where the tongue almost always
produces taste,
but so rarely provides truth.

CLYDE HURLSTON

CLOSE MY EYES

Can the veil upon intentions
Ever hide a form of grace?
Are the emotions we misplace
Best for another soul to taste?
Is deception just another word
For something we should guess?
Were our lives always destined to become
Such a fucking mess?
Questions cavalcade around me
As the ceiling's staring down
Sleep was never more elusive
Then when you are not around
The doubts mirror flooding waters
As the bed begins to rise
And the waters they never cease
Until I finally close my eyes
Are the answers ever lurking
Anywhere around the bend?
Have you finally lost your zeal
For playing out pretend?
Why do the roses that we love
Always have to come with thorns?
And why are the depths of angels
Only reached by those with horns?
Questions cavalcade around me
As the ceiling's staring down
Sleep was never more elusive
Then when you are not around
The doubts mirror flooding waters
As the bed begins to rise
And the waters they never cease
Until I finally close my eyes
Hello darkness my old friend
May this eternal night, it never end
For loyalty was another of their lies
It's only ever been you and me,
Each time I close my eyes

A BEAUTIFUL DOOM

Each time a spider makes its web
We should all share a bit of dread
For flies are anything but shy
When a certain scent is in their head
But who am I to raise my hand
As if I was ever able to understand
Why the things that truly last
Are so rarely built inside of sand
Questions cavalcade around me
As the ceiling's staring down
Sleep was never more elusive
Then when you are not around
The doubts mirror flooding waters
As the bed begins to rise
And these troubled waters never cease
Until I finally close my eyes
Hello darkness my old friend
May this eternal night, it never end
For loyalty was another of their lies
It's only ever been you and me,
Each time I close my eyes
I'll say hello again, my old friend
I swear the torment, it never really ends
For love was just another of her lies
It's only ever been you and me,
Each time I close my eyes.

CLYDE HURLSTON

SPELLING DOOM

I bore witness to your busy days,
I have watched them many times.
And I've placed patience intertwined with grace,
Into so many of my rhymes.
Hoping you could stop and smell the roses,
I once planted between these lines.
And remember all the love you received.
When you noticed the largest of the vines.
Which often grew to greet the sun,
Then attempted to bring you back its light.
And despite circumstances spelling doom,
He still cast you as the moon at night.
Yes, in every world you held his heart
With both tenderness and care.
Still, the tide would often rise and fall
Upon castles that were hastily erected there.
So to no surprise, much had washed away
By the time you did depart.
For erosion has been said to hollow out
That which was never solid from the start.
And we can blame my unsteady legs,
For the blatant trepidation in your own.
But at the end of truthful stories told,
It is I who is to blame, for ending up alone.

A BEAUTIFUL DOOM

END OF ACT I

"Rarely do we find men who willingly
engage in hard, solid thinking.
There is an almost universal quest
for easy answers and half-baked solutions.
Nothing pains some people
more than having to think."

- Dr. Martin Luther King, Jr.

"You can't change who you are,
but you can change what you have in your head,
you can refresh what you're thinking about,
you can put some fresh air in your brain."

- Ernesto Bertarelli

"In the egoic state, your sense of self, your identity, is derived from your thinking mind - in other words, what your mind tells you about yourself: the storyline of you, the memories, the expectations, all the thoughts that go through your head continuously and the emotions that reflect those thoughts. All those things make up your sense of self."

- Eckhart Tolle

II
MEMENTO AMARE

"Who, being loved, is poor?"

– Oscar Wilde

"If a thing loves, it is infinite."

– William Blake

"The greatest happiness of life
is the conviction that we are loved;
loved for ourselves, or rather,
loved in spite of ourselves."

- Victor Hugo

CLYDE HURLSTON

"THE DANGER OF BEAUTY" ART BY MITCH GREEN

A LOVE THAT RAGED

I once said to someone
that I have walls built up inside myself.
And these barriers, at a glance,
could possibly rival Everest if I let them.
And just beyond their face,
there lies this ocean of emotions.
A blackened sea; that I have often called
my fabled reservoir of words.
And in the past,
there was one who professed
a deep desire to swim; but sadly,
circumstances proved
that she was mistaken.
But then another came along;
and with one touch, she left within me
the modern ruins of Jericho.
And as the stones rained
down like tears of joy,
the seas of shimmering black raged;
and brought with them a love
that rivaled the wrath of the gods.
But alas, she too fell
victim to circumstance;
and returned to the safe harbor she knew.
And who could blame her?
For it's not everyday
that the epic of Gilgamesh comes to life.
And we are sometimes drowned
by the things we need the most.
So I do not curse her name.
I just hope the next Goddess
who enters this realm,
is twice the swimmer she became.

CLYDE HURLSTON

A ROYAL DILEMMA

What am I to do when the one
who took me to the clouds,
has placed me back upon the ground?
And left me here to sympathize,
with the tree that fell
and never made a sound?
See, I was always more concerned,
with her pain and not my own.
But now the one who called me
her handsome King,
has left me in this heavy chair alone.
And I'm forced to live without her smile,
when I'm in need of light.
Where is she to tell me that I am wrong,
when I am tired of being right?
How can the one who
caused the flames to dance,
forget to provide me with a spark?
How can the moon to my eternal tide,
choose to leave me in the dark?
Well, I guess she must survive
this wretched life,
in any way she can.
But I'll admit that I forget to breathe,
as I try to simply understand.
Still I'll never hate her for what she's done,
I hope she knows this to be true.
But there's an ache within my bones,
knowing their fix is overdue.
Yet withdrawals are commonplace,
in this kingdom fast decayed.
I just wish she knew how many nights,
I spent wishing that she stayed.

ANCHORS (PART 2)

I was long a slave to reason,
but then you did invade my rhyme.
Now things I used to live for,
feel like they were a giant waste of time.
I'd pretend that I existed,
as the apple of your eyes.
But the seeds of my suspicions,
have now borne fruit inside your lies.
Dear, was I your lover at the least,
or a distraction at the most?
'Cause the truth is hard to see,
since you became a ghost.
And now, I'm treading rougher seas,
so the end is getting close.
Just let me drown in peace,
come and take your anchors
out of my bones.

CLYDE HURLSTON

THE LATENT TRUTHS OF NATURE

She once asked me,
"baby, what's your greatest fear?"
My reply was, "losing you."
She laughed and said I was being crazy.
But she didn't realize that I already understood
the latent truths of nature.
See? I knew that once
a caged bird is released,
the first thing she will do is take to the sky.
And once she has tasted the morning light
pouring through the clouds like wine,
the last thing she will do
is trade that freedom for another cage;
or even another perch.
So you must be prepared
to lose her in the sun for good;
while hoping she desires to return.
Then remind yourself that your open arms
should never feel like a prison;
and when it comes to
matters of the heart or mind,
you must be prepared
to live with her decision.
Yet having said all of that,
you'll still have to find a way
to breathe without her.

BANISHED

The ends of the Earth
would've known my face,
if it would've helped
to earn your smile.
I've journeyed now
to hell and back,
and found success in every trial.
But now there is
no way for me to change,
this cemented course you've set.
For I've been banished to the wind,
by the one who's impossible to forget.

CLYDE HURLSTON

RESENT / RESEND

Darling,
when I look back
at the choices you've made,
I must admit
it is hard not to resent you.
But then the memories
come flooding back,
and it feels as if we
always pick things up
right where we left off.
And so I don't even stop
to wonder whether
it was Heaven or Hell
that decided to resend you.
I've missed you so fucking much,
that I don't even care if
your halo is hiding horns.

PRAYERS & SPELLS

Today, I heard a man speak of magic.
And in doing so,
he said something that
struck me as profound:
"Every thought is a prayer,
and every word is a spell."
Though before now, in my hubris,
I was inclined to scoff at such a thing.
But as I stand here today,
I'm more open-minded than I've ever been.
For how could I not be?
Have you seen her?
Surely, she is a gift that was made for me
to discover when I was ready.
The way that she looks at me,
makes me feel like I am Samson.
Yet when her focus lies elsewhere,
my ego curses her as Delilah.
But when I'm in her favor,
her words harden this part of me like steel.
Who could do such a thing without touch?
Tell me, is she not
the magic they once spoke of?
Does she not know
the power that she wields?
Oh, if she doesn't,
let my skin be the campus
upon which she will learn.
For if desire breeds the fire,
tell her she has me ready to burn.
And I'm counting the very days,
until I feel her hands,
and I can then be reduced to ash.

CLYDE HURLSTON

VESTIGES OF SLAVERY

Vestiges of you can still be found
dancing in my bloodstream...
Proving that every time I am awake,
I am still held captive by a dream.
The crescent moon belies its shine,
a truth your smile has shown.
I see you standing there amidst the ruins,
and I marvel at how you've grown.
As stones rained down
and some were thrown,
oh how you fought to persevere.
Driving blindly in the dark,
with your destination far from clear.
Still you found your way into the blue,
though the skies had fallen black.
And your foundation was standing tall,
despite displaying every crack.
As you rebuild with tired hands,
knowing you must work before you rest.
I wonder if you've come
to miss the serenade,
of this war drum
raging inside my chest.

BEFORE THE FORECAST

Tell me something darling...
When you close your eyes at night,
do I ever cross your mind?
Or maybe the question I should ask is,
did I ever have a place in there at all?
For at night I wonder,
as you embark
on this new journey of yours,
with a heart that's too big to hold,
and a grace that feels
much too out of place;
will you think of me?
Or are you so far removed
from the days when you reigned,
that you avoid your memories
like bad weather?
Surely, there must be something
that could still make you smile,
the way you did before
the forecast called for pain.
But I honestly don't know
if I want the answers to these questions.
Maybe taking the truth
right between the eyes,
is the fastest way to blindness.
Yet there's not a day that passes,
when I don't try to drown my hurt,
in a sea shaped like my pride.

CLYDE HURLSTON

THE GUILTY PARTY

Your sweet professions of friendship,
were given breath in vain.
And despite my many observations,
I won't bother to complain.
Because it's forever in your nature,
to waste my fucking time.
As you pander to the jury,
so you won't be convicted of the crime.
But worry not, little darling;
for this is not a trial.
No, this is just a hearing,
for each time I was in denial.
Since I was generous with second chances,
and still you burned each waiting bridge.
It feels like I was in the secret service,
taking fire from the ridge.
As you sped away to safety,
leaving much damage in your wake.
Leaving this foolish man to wonder,
how much more he could take.
But dear, you are a stranger to me,
I can say this without shame.
Never again will I allow
your wretched tongue,
to place a stain upon my name.
Because truthfully,
I'm the only guilty party,
for ever expecting you to change.

ESCAPE FOR THE REFUGE

In the past, I was a refuge;
a place where Queens
escaped from the burdens
of their crowns.
With me, there was
no need for pageantry;
so it was the floor that
often wore their gowns.
For my first,
I was too fleeting of a harbor;
she felt the seas weren't calm for long.
That's because I was
frightened by her worship,
for its magnetic pull was strong.
So I put my duty before my pleasure,
and I retreated to the tower.
But it was her who showed me how it felt,
when royalty wields its power.
And for the other, I was a King;
though it was briefly that I ruled.
I thought my reign would be eternal,
but her hands molded me into a fool.
And so I'm left here inside the wind,
staring intently to the North.
While finding memories
in this glass of rum,
since it was the Kraken
who brought them forth.

CLYDE HURLSTON

PAY HOMAGE

When you read these words,
you will know that
you still linger in my mind.
When you read these words,
you will know exactly
how much you meant to me.
When you read these words,
you will know that
no matter what you do,
you will never replace me.
No one will ever
make your heart race,
nor will they stir
your soul the way that I did.
No one will set a fire in you
that will burn brighter than ours did.
We were the envy of the Vikings.
They held funerals;
laying to rest the hopes
of finding a love like ours.
Another man may look at you,
and he may even love you;
but your body will not arch for him
the way it did for me.
You will not go about your days,
hiding your soreness,
knowing how deeply my love moved in you.
You may learn to say his name,
but you will never call him King
after he made you call for God.
So know this darling;
you may never be mine again;
but oh baby, you will belong to me forever.
And you can take that to the fucking bank.
So pay homage, baby.

BACKSEAT EXPERIMENTS (PART I)

Some days, I wonder if
our love was an experiment for her.
She often spoke highly of me
in conversations; so maybe she finally
worked up the nerve to test her hypothesis.
And who knew that my backseat
would become the laboratory?
I certainly didn't.
But what I do know is, that first touch?
My god, that was the greatest
chemical reaction there has ever been.
The second she placed her hand on my forearm,
and leaned in to kiss me,
I knew I'd never be the same again.
It was as if one added fluorine to hydrogen;
and the explosion sent shockwaves
barreling throughout the entirety of my life.
My love for her consumed me;
and the results were incalculable.
She invaded my thoughts, my dreams...
even my writing failed to be free of her.
How in the hell was I supposed to function?
How could I breathe if I was anywhere
but inside of her?
How could my world remain on its axis,
without her gravity to keep me whole?
And now that the tests are over,
what am I supposed to do now?
What good are results,
if no one wants to replicate them?

CLYDE HURLSTON

WINDOWS TO THE SOUL (PART II)

They say the eyes
are the windows to the soul;
and so, she often asked
to gaze into mine.
I wondered aloud, from time to time,
if she ever noticed just how
magnificent she looked in them.
Because, I knew how common
my brown eyes were in the world;
but in my heart, I knew that no one
looked at her the way that I did.
And that's not to say that these eyes
didn't see beauty in other places...
no, this world is too grand,
and too much of a miracle to be ignored.
Yet I could proudly say,
without hyperbole or exaggeration,
that I only had eyes for her.
The sound of her calling my name,
may as well have been a symphony;
since such a thing was music to my ears.
But these days, I must admit
the music is gone.
And so, I've chosen to focus
on improving my mind,
and even broadening my outlook.
Then I'll get around to the renovations
on this dilapidated temple.
But my heart?
That's as stubborn as its owner.
I'm not completely sure
if it will ever be open again.
But someone amazing has found me,
she's determined to remodel
the place that you used to own.
So in the end, I'm still a very lucky man.

AN UNSPOKEN WISH (PART III)

As a child, I would hear stories
of genies granting wishes.
If you were lucky enough to find their lamp,
a few well intentioned rubs,
would free the one who could
make your dreams a reality.
Even then, I struggled
to believe such things.
But then I met her;
and while there was no genie,
my wish definitely came true.
And while the circumstances
were far from ideal,
I could not deny that magic was for real.
Yet, these days I'm more alone
than I've ever been.
And who would've thought
that lightning could strike twice?
Because there is another goddess
who has found me; as I am
stumbling through my own path days,
drunk off of self-doubt and uncertainty.
Though my words may occasionally
inspire her reticence,
she still speaks my name with desire.
Though my actions occasionally
provoke her doubts,
she still craves my company.
So in the coming weeks, I will
journey to her temple,
and give myself to her.
Maybe her touch can save me,
from the darkness clawing at my thoughts.

CLYDE HURLSTON

MORE THAN BREATHING

He said to err was only human,
and that forgiveness was divine.
But I believe the former is only natural,
while the latter comes with time.
So what once had grown between us,
was sure to wither on the vine.
For death has no place within the universe,
if it's not conjoined with time.
So while you came to love me,
I knew there would be a day.
When your eyes forsook the spark in mine,
and you'd surely turn away.
Sure, circumstances played a part,
we both know this to be true.
But bitter truths have raised their heads,
when it comes to me and you.
See? I loved you more than breathing,
you loved not to be alone.
So that is why I'm sitting here
still fighting tears,
with only this pen to call my own.

WORLDLY DEEDS

I have my eyes set on a new moon;
yet I wonder if she sees.
How her words move me like the tide,
just as the wind does to the trees.
I wonder if she'll grace me with her light,
for I hope to make her smile.
I long to be worthy of her love,
and make this life worth her while.
Though my doubts are bound to stir,
I'll ignore them as best I can.
Because time will be sure to wash away,
these castles made of sand.
And I hope to be the kind of man,
she'll find it hard to live without.
Knowing that I'll only give her loving words,
without raising my voice to shout.
And I hope to be the kind of lover who'll,
turn her deepest wants to needs.
Because my only goal is her happiness,
when engaging in these worldly deeds.

CLYDE HURLSTON

THE VERY LAST DROP

After the back and forth
of our conversations,
I teeter on exhaustion.
It's hard work
restraining this passion of mine.
Sadly, at times, it is numb and lifeless.
But since her arrival,
the flames have begun to dance again.
So naturally my mind wanders...
Just a few seconds of hearing her voice,
I begin to wonder how her breath
will carry my name.
Just a few seconds of staring
at her photographs,
and I wonder how she will taste.
Will the stars dance upon our lips,
as she sends me out of this world?
How can a man describe the holy grail,
when he has yet to experience it?
Now that she knows what she does to me,
I wonder if she knows that
I don't want her to stop.
For I long to know what she holds within,
right down to the very last drop.
If she will have me...

HORRORS OF THE HEART

Staring out this window,
I have seen horrors of the heart.
The kind of things that would make
Darwin question his own theories.
Maybe it's not adaptability
that helps the fittest survive;
but rather, it's endurance.
Because the fastest creatures
can still be surprised,
and even the tallest creatures
are left without wings.
Yet can either of them suffer in silence?
Bleeding profusely without spilling a drop?
Because I've watched her do it.
On a daily basis.
And it amazes me what
human beings can become
accustomed to in this world.
Look at her...
how can such magnificence be overlooked?
How can someone who
takes my breath away,
wish that she was no longer breathing?
I watch with no answers;
and I wonder if my inaction
makes me worse than
the monster she still loves.

CLYDE HURLSTON

REVERBERATING LOVE

Her touch
still reverberates
on my skin.
Leaving these
ripples in my blood.

TRAVELER

When she said needed space,
friend I didn't think she meant the stars.
Otherwise I would've pulled them down,
and tried to capture them in jars.
Yet in the weeks her silence grew,
I often wondered if she mastered flight.
And since I felt her drift so far away,
I knew she wouldn't take the time to write.
Still I tried to understand...
Did she yearn for exploration?
Did she find much better sights to see?
Was there some form of freedom there
that she just couldn't find with me?
There were many nights I'd lie awake,
hoping to witness her return.
But on every night she'd disappoint,
leaving only lessons to be learned.
And the biggest one has been engraved,
right here upon my weary bones.
Travelers never truly come
to rest their hearts,
inside of broken or stifling homes.

CLYDE HURLSTON

NO TRESPASSING

I wonder if you'd ever claim
this cavern that she left behind.
This gaping hole within the heart
of a man that she used to call her home.
The hollow place now decorated poorly
with cobwebs and broken boards.
With rusted nails buried in places
that her fingertips used to kiss.
A once-welcoming doormat
carelessly replaced
with a "No Trespassing" sign.
The same sign that was eager
to come down when you
simply smiled in my direction.
Or did anything for that matter.
Darling, I wonder if
you marvel at her works,
and then remind yourself
that you could do far better
than she ever did. I wonder if you'll
ever see these smoke signals of mine
before they become sheep
amongst the clouds.
Sometimes I wonder if this
silence between us is you doing
your best impression of her.
Like that time she got rid
of the dead weight in her life,
that was shaped a lot like me.
Other times I wonder if your eyes
even look at me, the way mine look at you.
You know what? Come to think it…
Maybe I wonder too goddamn much.
It all feels pointless.

TREASURE MAP

I never remember how they begin,
but the end result is always the same.
You are the star of my dreams, darling.
The protagonist in my most vivid fantasies.
You have no idea the number of times,
I've imagined my large hand
lost inside your raven hair,
as I taste the passion upon the lips
that make my name sound like music.
I wonder if you could fathom
the countless nights, I've imagined
your body was a treasure map.
With your every tattoo
showing me a place that
I've dreamed of visiting with my tongue.
And you should know that
my memory fails to recall
a single second beneath the moon,
that I didn't lie awake,
with you spread out behind my eyes;
as I fucked you breathless
for as long as our bodies could take it.
It was always my honor to leave you wet
and shivering in a haze of our own creation.
But such thing was not meant
for the waking world...
Because you don't see me
the way I see you.
So I will have to suffer through my days
knowing I never got to leave you sore,
in all the places that my love could reach.

CLYDE HURLSTON

HER RADIANCE

There is an unmistakable glow,
that comes from a woman,
who was just made to cum.
After her muscles tightened,
and the air was harder to find
as she neared the summit,
after she is given her sweet release,
her radiance is the envy of the moon.
For her skin is electric to the touch;
and the ripples passing through her body
feel like waves sent from God.
Is there any wonder then,
that her walls come down,
and her hidden self comes alive?
It is in these moments that
inhibitions are made to forget her name;
and her primal needs must be met.
So she opens herself
to receive my love again.
Ever ravenous. Ever impatient.
She uses one hand to ready herself,
the other to place me inside of Eden.
She has seen the view
from her highest peak...
And if she is to return to that place,
she must have her valleys punished
in a fashion most proper.

A MEMOIR PENNED BY TIME

It seems as if the condition
grows worse by the day...
Despite constantly being left exposed,
and subject to the elements,
his skin held up quite well after all this time.
Even though it showed signs of wear,
if one were to look closely.
And as surely as each line told a story,
each scar and scab held their own place
in this memoir being penned by time.
Still, I can't help but wonder
if those who even bother to read
each proverbial page
in that metaphoric book,
will notice the common theme
running through all of the chapters:
how the starved find a way to survive.
For his skin longed for her touch,
in the way that plants reach for sunlight.
And because their times together
were sadly few and far between;
his imagination would be forced to try
and alleviate the ache
of both skin and soul.
But there's just no substitution
for her, dear reader.
So that is why he lies awake
in bed each night
hoping she will at least visit in dreams.

CLYDE HURLSTON

A LOVING DEMAND (PART I)

Come to me, darling...
With open mind
And open arms.
Come not out of pity,
But out of love.
And the fire inside these eyes
The passion in this heart
Will burn your skies
And brand them until they're blue.

AT YOUR OWN RISK (PART 2)

It seems that is the risk that we will take:
Will we prosper? Will we break?
Darling, there are some truths
that we cannot shake,
Here inside these respective beds we make.
Sure there is a risk,
But would your rather live or just exist?
Will you hide to avoid the flames,
I've seen no moth resist?
Or would you come home to burn,
And witness your inhibitions singe?
Knowing we'll produce a love more potent
Than the contents of any used syringe.

CLYDE HURLSTON

BACK TO LIFE

Tell me, what good are flames
without their source of provocation?
Tell me exactly, how they are to dance
when confined and
not given room to breathe.
I wonder, what good is a hypnotized moth,
when it's not blessed with
its favorite place to land?
Oh, how dare you, darling...
How dare you coax a soul to burn,
and not put it out before you leave.
How dare you leave a man
to breathe smoke,
and never again
get high upon the fumes.
How dare you stoke
coals within his dreams
and then mirror vapors
throughout the day.
You are something else, my love.
An arsonist, perhaps?
A vain and greedy temptress?
Or maybe, just maybe...
You're biding your time.
Letting more than
the temperature rise to new heights,
before you lie down upon your back,
and let the fire spread you open wide.
Come then, darling.
If you find yourself numb inside,
become my wet and waiting pyre.
And I will gladly burn you back to life.
Until you are singed of your desire
for any man but me.

A GIFT FROM THE GODS

Through the storm of existence,
the wholehearted find a way to endure.
Their intentions worn proudly
upon tattered sleeves,
as if to prove affiliation with The Seven.
And as they withstand the bombardment
of questions and the shrapnel of
assumptions, they find the strength
to dig deeply into this life.
With the hopes of
unearthing love, no less.
Their hands sadly come up empty
time and time again. And yet,
as the pendulum swings the other way,
it is the undeserving
who stumble upon good fortune.
Discovering a cache of priceless treasures
within the confines of one, single soul.
Given access to the depths of a temple
this leper could only pray
to from a distance.
And in their hubris,
their infantile carelessness...
they squander their gift from the gods.
Leaving me here to wonder,
what have I done wrong
to deserve such an eternal fate?
And can I make amends,
to maybe one day claim her for myself?

CLYDE HURLSTON

THE CREATION OF MORNING

Still to this day,
I believe the sun created the morning
just so it could see her smile.
And because I loved her,
I did my best to fight back the night;
to ensure she always had
enough room to shine.
But now, the sun has set
on her love for me;
and I don't know what to do.
Every attempt to find another
with a smile that would
bring me back to life, has proven futile.
Because of this,
I've stopped treading the hours,
and I've let the night overtake me.
Maybe in the darkness,
I'll discover that I cannot miss
what my eyes cannot see.

PRAYERS

She said,
"Clyde, I'm sorry
this has been so hard for you."
To which I replied,
"Darling, I'm sorry
that it hasn't been hard for you."
The heavy silence told me
that she understood:
It is easy for a soul to forget
that which was meaningless.
But for some,
It's impossible to forget
the one that was
the answer to their prayers.

CLYDE HURLSTON

MR. EXPERT

She said,
"Oh, stop it.
You're making me blush."
To which I naturally replied,
"You know what blushing
means don't you?"
"No, Mister Expert.
Why don't you tell me…"
"Well, darling,
blushing is your body's
natural response to something
that your heart always wanted to hear,
but your mind was convinced
that it never would."
"So why is my heart racing then?"
"Because you belong to me now.
Your search is over."

DOWN TO A SCIENCE

Darling, it seems that I've got
missing you down to a science...
I've mixed equal parts of hubris and regret.
Joining them were the ashes
of the bar you set,
that was high enough to kiss the sun.
Then I added a touch of hope
to the entirety of a passion gone dormant.
During the day, nothing happens.
But my god, at night?
They pool in my subconscious,
and quickly cause the same
uncontrollable reaction:
you invade my dreams.
Choking me on the fumes
of these erotic recollections.
Visions of lifting you off the ground,
until those three words
left your lips with haste.
Now without you here,
all of these ingredients go to waste.
What am I to do now?
I finally found the one distilled to perfection,
and alas she is gone from me.
Leaving me here with desired results
I will never duplicate again.

CLYDE HURLSTON

FLUID DESIRES

I've learned that for some,
their desires are as fluid
as their loyalties.
And they'll find themselves
beside, beneath, or on top
of another person
whenever it suits them best.

THE MYSTERIES OF DESIRE

Tell me, what is it like to be desired?
To know that your face
decorates their every thought...
What's it like to know that your presence,
your touch would be the remedy
for another's lonely night?
Do you like knowing that you
put the movement in their hand,
when the thoughts become too much?
Do you revel knowing
they produce explosions in your honor?
Or is it just noise for you?
I wonder how you feel about such things.
But more importantly,
I wonder how it would feel to be with you.
Whether it was forever or just a night.
For there has been at least
a thousand times that I've wondered
how it would be, to finally be inside of you.
To know your kiss, to know your taste.
To know how deeply I'd have to go,
to learn your combination.
So that I may unlock your desires
with just a look, and then unfold you
when we were finished.
But I fear these questions
may go eternally unanswered.
And it's such a shame.
Because you've taken my imagination
to its very base, darling.
But the only thing of yours I have ever felt...
Has been your silence.

CLYDE HURLSTON

"A COSMIC RIDE" ART BY MITCH GREEN

BEAST WITHIN

Within every man there lies a beast...
And there are only a few things
that will draw it out:
The unbridled rage
from a discussion turned argument.
The wanton violence
needed to quell any impending threat
to the ones he loves.
The prideful desire to be the victor
in any form of competition.
And the lustful moans of his woman
as she receives the pleasure he delivers.
You must take care
to only wake the side of the beast
that you wish to see.
Because when there is red
inside of a man's eyes,
he is liable to do anything.
And so one mustn't rattle his cage,
unless they are ready
to face the consequences.
But from the look inside your eyes,
I can tell it's been a long time
since you were ravaged properly.
Go on then, darling...
Tempt the beast behind my eyes.
Just don't say I didn't warn you.

CLYDE HURLSTON

BEFORE THE MORNING SUN

I've been waiting to see
that look in your eyes for too long, darling.
The look that tells me that
something aches deep within you,
and your hands just cannot reach it.
That is when the animal takes over,
and I demand you lie back,
so that I may spread you open
like my favorite book.
After a taste and the use of my fingers,
there is little doubt that
you are indeed ready for me.
And as those perfect legs
that carry you are bent back toward you,
my firm and pulsing love
finds its way inside.
While driving it deeper,
my ears are greeted by a serenade
of your pleas for persistence.
But as each gentle crash
becomes more thunderous,
you will feel the pain
of your requests tomorrow.
And despite my savage nature
during your internal calisthenics,
I take pride in knowing that
both of us will come
long before the morning sun;
so let us finish together.

FELT IN THE HEAVENS

They say that I was
supposed to be over you by now.
All of the signs say that I was
supposed to be moving forward;
yet it seems that I'm still stuck.
But, the gods know I've tried;
and by now, they know I'm tired.
Surely they can feel my anger,
even there amongst the heavens...
Having witnessed the holes
my fists have made in walls
because your name still
takes up real estate behind my eyes.
Knowing that I've died inside
every time I realized that
the hands upon your holy temple
would no longer be my own.
Knowing that I'm now forced
to place these memories
into a reliquary six feet deep,
just to get through the goddamn day.
And yet, you continue dancing
silent in my peripheries.
A not so subtle reminder
of the perfection I once possessed;
and lost when I wasn't looking.
May the gods forgive me...
I'm finally starting to hate you.

CLYDE HURLSTON

TRANSPARENT GODDESS

I swear, you are such
a fucking liar, darling...
I can recall all of
your proclamations
with a diamond's clarity;
but for the life of me,
I just cannot forgive you
for the dishonesty.
In my heart, these lies are insults;
and may as well be cardinal sins.
For someone who has professed
a love for the depths of my mind,
you sure have foolishly forgotten
its power when provoked.
The subtle changes in your behavior
are but aberrations to some;
but in my eyes, they are
the death throes of
the goddess you used to be.
I find no passion in your words now;
just hollow greetings
intertwined with recycled compliments.
You've become transparent
and your true colors
are bleeding through.
And that's the last thing
you and my heart
will ever have in common:
the bleeding.

YOUR PLACE OF REVERENCE

Darling, you will never know
how frustrating it is,
to write of you this way.
Whether I want to or not,
doesn't really seem
to matter to the gods.
For each time that
the inspiration finds me,
it often arrives with
pieces of you in tow.
So it leaves me here,
looking like a fool;
whilst trying to write you
a clear and direct path
back into my waiting arms.
And despite this strategy
clearly not working,
the ink continues to flow.
As others wish to occupy,
your place of reverence.
And she would always reply
with the same question...
"Why don't you let them, then?"
And since she never understood
the depths to which I felt for her,
my answer was always the fucking same:
"Because they are not you."
Her reply was always silence.

CLYDE HURLSTON

WILL THE FEVER BREAK?

I saw you curse the many shallows,
so I offered you my depths.
But I never knew that it would lead,
to the wasting of my breaths.
For you only seem to come around,
whenever there's a need.
Knowing my heart would provide the fertile ground,
in which you'd plant a seed.
Watching as it'd take root between the beats,
that sounded like your name.
While branches bearing fruit endure,
their respective guessing games.
Like which will be the next to fall,
right into your hands.
As you tell a tale as old as time,
leaving the glass to catch the sands.
Still I find myself ignored,
until you come crashing back.
Full of smoke to blow but lacking fire,
so indirect is your attack.
On heartstrings you choose to pull,
ensuring there'll be damage in your wake.
Proving that your selfishness,
is a fever that never breaks.

WHEN THE BEAST BEGINS TO STIR

You have left me here in wonder,
to hunger for an age.
And with no other place to turn,
you must be devoured on the page.
So as the night descends,
like spilled ink upon the stars.
I'm growing more impatient,
so this beast paces behind the bars.
But you see fit to provoke,
while leaving me only with a taste.
When you know
it's your fears and inhibitions,
that I would gladly lay to waste.
Just open up that door,
and I will rush in like the tide.
And sink my teeth into you,
to provide the sweet pain
you've been denied.
Oh, my little martyr,
won't you exchange
your cross for this bed.
And each thrust will coax from your lips,
the words you have never said.
And as you slowly realize,
that your fate is crystal clear.
Remember it was your actions,
that earned this punishment severe.
For as I move inside you with a vengeance,
my anger has taken hold.
And your temple sounds like the ocean,
despite my broad shoulders being cold.

CLYDE HURLSTON

PLAYING THE LAMB

I have wasted so much time
with my head in the clouds,
that I've been reckless
when pouring my truths on to pages.
I have placed women
high upon pedestals,
and then foolishly wonder
why they fail to see me.
Like a child, I was so proud
of this heart upon my sleeve,
I wanted to give it to
almost every pretty woman
who was kind to me;
not realizing that even poetry
can smell of desperation.
So it's no surprise when
moons that once
moved me like the tide,
have disappeared
behind darkened clouds,
never to be seen again.
Goddesses once worshipped
on paper and on breath,
have been proven themselves
to be the mere mortals
they always said they were.
And once angels displayed
their wings in vain, I knew that
I wasn't made for the Heavens.
That's when was forced
to come back down to Earth,
so that I may tear down
the monuments I once raised
as the offerings of a lonely man.
Never again shall I worship;
for my soul has grown too tired
of playing the lamb.

SAY YOU LOVE ME

If I had a dollar for all the times,
these walls have heard my screams.
That I would be a wealthy man,
and rich beyond my wildest dreams.
But if you were to look at my current state,
you'd see that wasn't true.
For the only thing of value here,
is this thing I have with you.
Since every night I find you,
you're right inside my bed.
And you help to make sense of things,
that often rattle 'round my head.
And it's then you get on top,
and I feel your perfect weight.
Then you take me deep inside of you,
because you no longer wish to wait.
And the tightness of your embrace,
always alleviates my fears.
Which frankly feels so fucking good,
my eyes fight to hold their tears.
And so you have your way with me,
and I'm left to wonder why.
My demons love telling me,
it'll be this way until I die.
But I do my best to ignore their taunts,
since that's all they seem to do.
I bet they've grown jealous of the way,
I feel when I'm with you.
So won't you say you love me, Silence?
Say it until you're out of breath.
Because every time I take a look around,
I see you're the only one who has never left.
And I'm learning to love you for that...

CLYDE HURLSTON

IN CASE OF EMERGENCY

You mistook her kindness
for a spark, didn't you?
You actually believed that
because you had things in common,
there'd be enough ground
to build a foundation, right?
When are you gonna learn, man?
Nobody wants you in that way.
Get with the fucking program already.
I mean, take a look around.
You're the shoulder to cry on,
the sympathetic ear.
Actually, you're the glass
they break in case of emergency.
You could drop dead tomorrow,
and they'd be none the wiser.
You might as well be a pallbearer
for your own heart, at this rate.
And I know you don't believe me.
Why would you?
You're too busy holding on
to hope; like a good, little fool.
You haven't even noticed
how she makes it a point to call you friend.
Your pet name was put to sleep, stupid.
She'll be beneath some other guy
eventually, while you'll be at home.
Trying to hold it together.
With a bank account and a pair of hands
that are emptier than your bed.
But hey, what do I know?
I'm just the voice inside your head.

I WOULD FALL FOR YOU

No matter what I could have ever said,
the truth was staring squarely in my face.
The same way the heart upon my sleeve,
was held so firmly in its place.
You see darling, I knew I would fall for you,
when I kept finding reasons to engage.
And I knew I would fall for you,
when one word replies felt constrictive like a cage.
Dear, I would feel incomplete when
your name didn't flash across my phone.
And I could be in a room full of people; still,
it was your silence that made me feel alone.
Yes, I knew I was in deep trouble then,
no I didn't have to guess.
And as I broke the speed of sound,
I knew there was no changing this.
Because the clouds were zooming by,
and there was no one to slow me down.
Eventually, I knew for sure,
I would have to kiss the ground.
For I never lacked any of my common sense,
I knew exactly how this would end.
But since I was proud to play the fool for you,
I never once bothered to pretend.
Yet, you found the strength to turn away,
as if you couldn't bear to see.
The way I died like Christ upon Mount Calvary,
knowing you had forsaken me.
I guess even after all of this time,
out of sight still means
out of mind for you, my love.
How fitting...

CLYDE HURLSTON

THE COURAGE OF STRANGERS

Another day,
another potential lover lost.
Most think I simply write away;
unaware of how much
these lines weigh until they cost.
But in the end, it matters not, dear reader.
For I've said before,
inspiration is a cruel mistress;
and it takes many of my pages to feed her.
I just wish those I once wrote about
would have kept the courage of strangers.
After all, it seems it was the mystery
and the sleight of hand that got them wet.
But sadly, this writer would remain
something they were rushing to forget.
Whether they'd admit it or not.

THE MONSTER THAT MEN MADE

They blamed the current climate.
They blamed an old political ideology,
being pushed through a myriad of ways.
They blamed the secular nature of society.
And they even went so far,
as to blame inanimate objects...
Such as crocheted vagina hats,
and supposed participation trophies.
And while there are some kernels of truth,
to be found in these obfuscating arguments;
many of those who are claiming themselves
to be awakened to the ills of hypergamy,
have done every single thing
but take a long look in the mirror.
For there is, sadly, a battle of the sexes
being waged throughout the world.
To the benefit of the elites.
And women didn't start it.
They are simply picking up the stones
that were thrown over the centuries,
and aiming them back
at the glass houses that cast them.
You see, we men tend to forget,
that many of these angry, modern women
are the monsters that men made.
Whether through neglect or abuse,
or through insincerity or infidelity.
Whether through objectification
or fear of their eventual education.
Women have suffered for a long time.
And now, the good must suffer for the bad.
And good men have to risk
being turned into stone,
for gazing into eyes made to water
by actions that were not their own.

CLYDE HURLSTON

"MEDUSA" ART BY MITCH GREEN

FOR SALE BY OWNER

There are valuable lessons
to be learned when one experiences
the loss of love; and it seems
most of us learn the hard way.
We discover, how rarely
selfless efforts are mirrored by another.
We learn that for some,
falling in love is far more exciting
than staying in love.
They yearn for the feeling
of weightlessness
and not the gravity of compromise.
And lastly, I've learned that
some of us have relationships,
while others have real estate.
When the space beside them
becomes vacant,
they easily fill it with someone else.
Possibly a client that
was already in the market.
And they can close the deal
and move on as if
nothing ever stood there;
as if nothing ever happened.
But for those of us
who were building our dreams with them,
the demolition takes a toll;
and the replacement leaves a hole.
Sure, things will get better in time.
But it's hard to get over the fact
that the one we held the most dear,
was over the loss
before the smoke was even clear.
Oh, how it hurts; bleeding in plain sight.

CLYDE HURLSTON

AND SHE WISHED…

And she wished to be a rainbow,
shining bright for all to see.
Here I thought she was the moon,
shining brightly just for me.
But she wants be a rainbow,
so she can be noticed by the soul.
Who will love her every color,
as she fights to heal and become whole.
Yeah, she wished to be the rainbow,
that was seen without the rain.
Since her most recent days,
were often filled with pain.
But now the clouds have moved,
and she can see the sun.
So she wants to be the rainbow,
that proves the storm is done.
Lord, to some she'll be the rainbow,
but to me she was the treasure at the end.
Because she was once the moon,
and I was the tide she said was just a friend.
Still, I wish her happiness in the skies.

THE ECSTASY IN AGONY

What was once said in ten lines,
Can now be said in one.
'Cause a love that
would have lived forever,
Is all so clearly done.
The heart's power is
measured with its beats,
Not the amount it bleeds.
So maybe my sacrifice upon each page,
Was not the sign she needs.
How else then, am I to show,
The ecstasy in my agony?

CLYDE HURLSTON

THE ONE I'VE BECOME

It's always at night
that she comes to visit.
She never knocks;
fearing that she will alert
others to her presence.
She wants me all to herself, you see?
Like the night descending
slowly upon the day,
she finds her way into my bed.
Before I know it,
she has her hands around my throat.
I never know what to say
in these instances;
her attempts are appreciated,
but they seldom work.
She doesn't have to touch me
to keep me in her grasp;
after all, she isn't a very loyal lover.
All you have to do is stop talking,
and she'll spread herself
wide open for you.
Her name is Silence.
She only comes here to hold me down,
so that her sister Solitude
can have her way with me.
Together, they cover me in loneliness.
And after every forced orgy,
I'm left more hollow than before.
Not even self-stimulation
helps to cure the numbness.
And so I wonder
what is the bigger mess:
the one they've left behind
or the one that I've become?

THESE SORE EYES

Here I go again,
a humble ocean resuming
its constant churning in the darkness.
Trying hard to mask my excitement,
now that the moon has resurfaced
and moved to another part
of the night sky. I swear she's still
a sight for these sore eyes.
And so, I watch with bated breath,
hoping she remembers the way
she used to shine;
so that she may guide my way
with her majestic light.
She has to see how I rise and rise;
falling forward every time.
Stumbling proudly
and trying my best
to reach the unattainable.
I know I'll never touch her;
but I'll be goddamned if I ever stop trying.

CLYDE HURLSTON

OUR COMBINED HEARTS

I guess it's true that
old habits die hard, darling.
Because I saw a picture
of you the other day;
and you looked so fucking good
I just had to save it.
And after tracing it with
my fingertips countless times,
I couldn't help but wonder
what could have been.
For I truly believe the smoke
our combined hearts produced,
just might have choked the cosmos.
But alas, it was not to be;
although, I'll never regret trying.
Still, when all is said and done,
I thought it was best I delete that picture.
Because the last thing
a recovering fool like me needs,
is more flammable material.
Otherwise, I may just discover
another way to burn for you.
Which would end up
being detrimental to me.
Especially since the past has proven,
there is no one more skilled
at ignoring the flames than you.

SPADES OVER HEARTS

Some will say that love
Is just a game that many play
Well you can use my life as proof
That I have never been that way
For when I give away my heart
The intent is for all of my days
But it seems it always ends
With my pieces in these graves
So now I'll raise the spade
And drive it deep into the dirt
Maybe then I can start to heal
This never-ending hurt
And though it seems I'm cursed
There's no choice but survive
But I hate that I'm mourning you
And it's because you're still alive
Some will say that time
Has the strength to heal our wounds
But I've been bleeding out
For so very many moons
And by the gods I wish
This pain would choose to spare
The soul who's only crime
Was showing true love and care
But now I'll raise the spade
And drive it deep into the dirt
Maybe then I can start to heal
This never-ending hurt
And though it seems I'm cursed
There's no choice but survive
But I hate that I'm mourning you
And it's because you're still alive
Oh, if giving all I had to give
Was the cardinal kind of sin
Then friend I'm afraid to say
That I will proudly sin again
For I know of no other way

CLYDE HURLSTON

To share this internal light
So let this dirt shower me
And bring on the endless night
Because now I will raise this spade
And drive it deep into the dirt
Maybe then I can start to heal
This never-ending hurt
And though it seems I'm cursed
There's no choice but survive
I just hate that I'm mourning you
And it's because you're still alive.

Yes, I hate that I'm here
mourning you, my love…
And it's because you're still alive.

NO WARNINGS FROM THE MOON

Our love was a castle:
made of sand,
recklessly erected
upon the shores of time.
And each passing day
was another greedy wave,
seeking to steal
just a little bit more of us.
Oh, how I wish
the moon had warned me,
I'd be fighting the tides alone.

CLYDE HURLSTON

SERVED, WITH LOVE

She looked up at me,
with those eyes that held me captive
more times than I can count,
and she asked me to say her name.
"Why," I asked;
unable to hide my confusion.
"Because I want to hear
if it sounds like a chore to you,
or if there is pride in your voice
when you say it," she replied.
Feeling as if she was
now one-up on me.
So I simply smiled
and leaned forward,
then I whispered her name into her ear.
Her eyes met mine, not a second later.
And they couldn't hide
her disappointment.
"I knew it. I knew you
weren't proud of me" she said.
Trying to hide the crack in her voice.
"No, darling.
That's not why I whispered.
You never did understand
the depths of this love I have for you.
I whispered your name for one reason..."
"Oh yeah? What's that?" she asked.
"Because that's the way God heard it
every single night,
when I actually prayed
and I asked him for what I wanted most."
It was then her perfect lips fell open,
and a gasp escaped their grasp.
As I got up to leave the room,
knowing I had finally gotten my point across.

TREAT ME LIKE A PAGE

After making it through several pages
of my Sacred Gift, she put the book down
as quickly as she could.
And with the look in her eyes,
I could tell she was up to something.
I guess my words must have had
an effect on her. So she quickly made
her way out of her bed,
and over to the large chair I was sitting in.
She then sat on my lap,
and leaned forward.
Placing her perfect lips right by my ear,
she whispered: "I want you
to treat me like one of your pages."
"Does this mean you want me
to place you on my desk,
and have my way with you?"
"No," she said; as she draped my
left arm across her shoulders.
"I want you to hold me down with this hand,"
she whispered, as she placed
my left hand on her throat.
Then she took my right hand
off of her thigh, and placed it
inside of her panties.
Letting me feel just how wet she was.
"And now that you have this hand
between the margins," she said,
while kissing my neck.
"Be a good writer
and make a mess out of me.
Use those large fingers
and take me to Heaven again."
And as the first finger disappeared,
quickly followed by the second;
her wish was my command.

CLYDE HURLSTON

A PRAYER FOR THE LAST TIME

Darling, you have no idea the restraint
it takes for me not to tell you
about these thoughts I have of you.
Specifically, the first time.
That long, overdue first time
I will have you all to myself.
In my mind, my fingertips
have explored your soft skin,
more times than I can count.
I've envisioned the goosebumps
rising up to greet my fingers,
like a message from the gods written in braille,
for only my heart to read.
And if you knew the many times,
I've fantasized about decorating
the inside of your thighs with kisses,
I fear you may think that tasting you
is the only thing I want to do in life.
But causing your eyes to widen,
from the efforts of my tongue
would just be the start of the night, my love.
We haven't even gotten to the best part...
The penetration.
My hardened love has been knocking
at the gates of Eden the entire time,
my mouth was exorcising your demons;
and so it was time you let me in, baby.
And oh fuck, you let me all the way in.
You welcome me so slowly,
I feel your fingernails
bury themselves in my skin,
as you greet me by the inch.
And there it is, my love.
I'm all the way to the base.
Your lips part to gasp;

but the depths I've reached,
have taken your breath away.
So I kiss you... tasting the joy in your silence.
And with each subsequent thrust,
you make a home for me within you.
First within your sacred garden,
and then within your precious heart and soul.
All because from the first wall I hit,
you can tell my aim isn't just destruction;
but rather, I aim to heal the parts of you
I am unable to leave wet and sore.
I've loved you long before I've fucked you.
You've just been too scared to let me in until tonight.
Afraid of what you friends would think.
Afraid of what your family would think.
Afraid of what your self might think.
All because I am admittedly,
not yet what I fully need to be.
So while I may not yet look the part,
I will reach that eternal goal,
given how well you can take the part.
So all of that fear can't save you now, darling.
You're mine now.
And I am on the path.
The path to becoming the three-eyed lion.
And then you can imagine
all we will become and all the places
we will come together in the years that follow.
But for tonight, the poetic beast
residing between your legs
and pounding his love
into paradise will have to suffice.
Because while you are busy moaning,
and calling out for God,
he will be fighting to hold back the tides of love,
and he will be praying.
Praying that this first time together,
will be the very last time,
you ever want to feel the love of a man who is not him.
Because that means you'll be his forever.

CLYDE HURLSTON

HOLY WATERS

Darling,
every single step I take
back toward the light,
is taken with you in mind.
For despite all that has changed,
and all that will change,
some things for me
remain the same.
And that is why
once my healing is done,
I pray that I am blessed
with the ability to journey
into your holy waters.
For I believe
with all of my heart,
that you may just be
the answer to my prayers.

A BEAUTIFUL DOOM

END OF ACT II

"Love has nothing to do with what you are expecting to get–only with what you are expecting to give which is everything."

- Katharine Hepburn

"Love is a fire. But whether it is going to warm your hearth or burn down your house, you can never tell."

- Joan Crawford

"Love makes your soul crawl out from its hiding place."

- Zora Neale Hurston

"Being deeply loved by someone gives you strength, while loving someone deeply gives you courage."

- Lao Tzu

III
MEMENTO MORI

"The meaning of life is that it stops."

- Franz Kafka

"Everybody is going to be dead one day, just give them time."

- Neil Gaiman

"I'm the one that's got to die
when it's time for me to die,
so let me live my life the way I want to."

- Jimi Hendrix

CLYDE HURLSTON

"DEATH ARRIVES EVENTUALLY." ART BY MITCH GREEN

FACE THE DEPTHS

I'm finding peace within your silence,
seeking wonders in the abyss.
Pondering all of the fleeting sounds,
that I will barely miss.
So please continue showing me,
the frozen shoulder that you own.
'Cause my stance has grown
more than bolder,
as I face the depths alone.

CLYDE HURLSTON

WHEN THE CLOUDS COME

It's that time of night again.
Sleep has resumed being its elusive self.
Reminding me of the futility
of trying to hold water in my hands.
And it's in these times,
where loneliness often fights
to try and take the wheel.
But tonight, I'd rather not
go down that road for the millionth time;
so I'll bid my wishful thinking
to drive for once.
And while part of me wants to journey
to the alternate universes I once spoke of,
the other part of me would rather
find something in the here and now.
So yes, the endless search continues.
For now my heart
is just a curious passenger;
and it's my pragmatic mind
with its foot upon the gas.
Maybe one day,
someone will catch up to me
and remind me what royalty feels like.
But until then, this road will have to do.
Because for me,
martyrdom has lost its luster;
and solitude is just a pretty word
for dying alone.
And for once,
I would rather burn violently with life.
So much so,
that on the days when the clouds come,
I will instead feel like the sun.

SENTENCE OF SOLITUDE

When staring down the sands of time,
one must speak honestly of their fate.
And so despite what
beautiful words others may offer me,
I have accepted this
life sentence of solitude.
Because in all of my years
of observation from the tower,
I've learned a great and many things.
For instance, I've discovered that
a valiant effort does not
always yield results.
Through dismay, I've witnessed
how broken people will often find the means
to remain within their maelstroms.
And at the expense of love,
I've experienced the ways that royalty
will eventually tire of gold;
and the gods will grow weary of worship.
That is why you should never bother
pouring all of yourself into another soul.
Why should you bleed to give them rain,
when the vast majority of them
deserve the fucking drought?
Leave them to their own devices...

CLYDE HURLSTON

UNWELCOME REVELATIONS

Why must unwelcome revelations,
always cause a world to end?
And why does a kiss before betrayal,
have to be the constant trend?
It seems I've failed to see the many times,
the pale horse began to ride.
Was it just denial on my part?
Or was I blinded by my pride?
Sitting here amongst the ruins,
I wonder if any of this was real.
Because her love doesn't seem to live,
in any place that I can feel.
Still I'm expected to hold my tongue,
and not curse her once golden name.
While knowing that the sweet
has given way,
to both bitterness and shame.
How many of us shall play the fool,
with her spear buried into our side?
And nine inch nails inside our wrists,
bleeding love until we've died?
But I'm sure she'd claim she'd resurrect,
the one who earned her love.
Yet here I thought I was the holy one,
that she would place no other soul above.
My god, how wrong I was...

WEIGHTLESSNESS

When it comes to love,
being unique is not a
prerequisite for reverence.
One should never assume
that the mirrors will reflect
all that you've shown them.
Most people aren't
prepared to till the Earth,
and give their roots a place to rest.
No, they seek new lovers with haste.
And so they'd much rather live
with their heads in the clouds,
than to spend any time on the ground.
Because to them, solitude is torture.
Leading them to find a new toy,
to occupy their minds and hearts.
And fresh passions help them
ignore the cracks within themselves.
But once that shine has lost its luster,
and the intoxication of discovery
has worn off, they will decide to
destroy and rebuild somewhere else.
Because in the end,
there are those who don't enjoy
the work of being in love.
They merely long
for the weightlessness of falling.
So do yourself a favor:
don't ever catch them.

CLYDE HURLSTON

NO REST FOR THE WEARY

My, how these
brown eyes have grown weary...
Having witnessed the evisceration
of youth by time,
and knowing that just beyond them,
the inquisition is eternal and ongoing.
For the questions, they never stop.
They often come in waves;
eroding the bedrock
of certainty I once possessed.
I've reached the point in life,
where nothing or no one
is beyond contestation.
The burdens of perspective
throw the scales
of importance into disarray;
and here I stand in the maelstrom,
fighting to salvage sense
where none has been found to lie.
Leaving conviction to feel more like
imprisonment than confidence.
What am I to do
when treading water feels like dying,
and drowning feels like relief?
I guess I'll flail these arms for today,
and leave tomorrow to be dealt with then.

THE WALKING CONTRADICTION

In all of the animals of nature,
it is man that is the most savage.
With his seemingly inherent need
to fight, to feed, and to fuck
his way through existence.
His ego, a deep-seated emotional phallus,
waved at anyone who would dare
to gaze upon his works.
Yet, this prideful beast walks upright.
With opposing thumbs
and in possession of
an intellect so profound,
that he can contemplate his origins.
He loves knowing he has both
the ability to create and to destroy.
To compose and to paint;
to write and to dance.
His abilities seems endless.
But how can one explain
such a conspicuous dichotomy?
Are the hands of Janus
involved in such a thing?
Is this merely polarity at work?
I often wonder,
can these opposing sides
ever truly be reconciled?

CLYDE HURLSTON

WHOSOEVER HOLDS THIS HAMMER

Despite our selfish desires,
the truth remains a hammer.
On its own, it is balanced.
Being neither good nor evil,
the hammer simply is.
Yet when grasped
and coupled with intention,
the truth becomes a weapon.
Possessing the ability to both
build another soul,
and destroy them on a whim.
This is why we must
take care of our truths,
no matter the cost.
Because if there is an empire
that can be torn down
with no more than a hammer,
then my friend, it doesn't deserve
to stand for a single second longer.
Because the truth must always
come to the light;
and the hammer has two ends
to hold all souls accountable.
For whatever can be done with you,
can be done to you.
Behold as its power drives us all.
For some, that will be forever forward.
And for others?
It will drive them into the ground.
So choose wisely.

A TONGUE HELD IN VAIN

These days I find myself
having to hold my tongue;
not out of fear mind you,
but out of respect.
The current paradigm
some have placed themselves in,
doesn't allow room for one such as I.
The ocean behind my eyes,
and the war drum inside my chest
aren't welcome within the confines
of their lives any longer.
These gorgeous souls,
that once could whisper and
effortlessly harden my love like granite,
barely say anything in my direction now.
Meanwhile, the others keep their distance
out of self-preservation.
And that is fine; such is their right.
I truly wish them nothing
but the best this life has to offer.
But I'm often left to wonder
if I have ever made my mark in this life.
Does my name still make a spark
within them, the way it once did?
Or was I merely striking stones alone,
when they first stumbled upon me?
I don't know anything for certain anymore.
All one can do is hope.

CLYDE HURLSTON

CURSE THE NAME

I've come to curse the name
of those who willingly choose
to squander their gifts;
especially if that name is mine.
Because this world is daily
being drowned by darkness,
and there are those of us
whom I believe have been chosen.
To not only bear but
bravely share the light;
for even the smallest of embers
are not our own to hoard.
We must do our collective best
to shine and help others
find the path to their own sovereignty.
We cannot allow the glow
of good souls to go dim,
simply because we haven't
paid attention to them
in this morally bankrupt society.
Because the stakes are too high
and the odds not in our favor.
But I bid you to take a look back
in history, and ask yourself:
When has that ever stopped us?

DEPRESSION'S DREAMS

There were times in the past
that I used to want to die.
Not by my own hand;
but as long as the goal was achieved,
I truly didn't care.
But looking back, as I often do,
I realize now that those were
depression's dreams and not my own.
The Earth can bring me comfort,
but not by being inside of it.
And now, hearing so many people I love
wish the same fate upon themselves,
makes me want to grab life
by the fucking throat.
Demanding that it give them back
their peace, before I burn
the whole world down.
But I remind myself that
I can't desire life for them;
all I can do is squeeze
every drop from my own.
And maybe, just maybe,
it will be worth it in the end.
For I refuse to let the darkness win.

CLYDE HURLSTON

PAINT THE OCEAN RED

These days,
contemplation feels
like a hollow practice.
My mind is an ocean;
and I'm the shipwrecked fool
cursed to drift within it.
I can't tell you the exact date
I went into the waves,
but I do know that I've been
treading water ever since.
Some days,
I dream of resting my arms
and becoming
acquainted with the depths;
but then I remember
what dry land used to feel like,
and it helps me to swim a little longer.
But then the memories start invading;
just like her majesty's fabled armada.
Their ships stretching as far
as the eye can see.
Their sails the envy of the clouds,
attached to masts
that grew to kiss the sun.
They mock me by using cannons
shaped like her face;
and for my resistance,
I'm soon obliterated
by all I used to crave.
Where once I would've died
to make her smile,
now I paint this ocean red,
and she's nowhere to be found.
Which serves me right;
for believing her,
when she claimed she felt the same.

BECOME ROYAL

It is time.
Do you hear me, self?
It's time.
Time for you to pick up the pieces
and get on with your goddamn life.
You know there are
far more pressing matters at hand.
Yes, I know you're angry.
You have every right to be.
But don't you think it's time?
No, don't let that rage go.
Just channel it into something better.
Improve yourself. Stop talking about it
and daydreaming about it.
Start today.
Long journeys can be
made with small steps.
Walk before you run. Just start moving.
Stop wasting time on memories.
Remember that nature burns the forest
down before things can grow again.
Teach yourself to hate her,
so you can remember
how to love yourself.
Then you'll become who you already
thought you were:
a fucking King in your own skin.
So from this day forth,
let no one question you.
Not friends. Not family.
Not perspective lovers.
Not even yourself.
Stay loyal, but become royal.

CLYDE HURLSTON

PERSPECTIVE

If only I could see myself
The way that others see me.
Maybe then this perspective
Would feel more like a crown,
And less like a cross.

DREAD TO DRAW

Darling, dreams for me
were but temporary highs.
Drugless, sleep-induced stupors...
in which logic was suffocated
beneath the weight of a hope
this life never justified.
Now, I curse those momentary delusions;
in which I nightly, sometimes daily,
bathed my curiosity.
Wondering why I used to imagine
what it would be like, even if it was only
for the duration of a breath,
to be considered normal...
But such a thing was never meant
for souls like me.
The hollow halls of this tower
were tailor-made for me and
this face and frame
both designed for shadows.
I was a fool to believe I had a place
carved out beneath the sun;
or worse yet; forever beside the moon.
The blackest of clouds
were the only accent upon the skies
I'd dread to draw. "Look for the light
at the end of the tunnel," they'd say.
Forgetting that mine got up
and walked the other way.
Now, I have no choice but to
build a castle in the lasting shade.
For there are times when surface life,
feels just like a grave.

CLYDE HURLSTON

IN THE PERIPHERIES

Darling, are there days
when you feel like God?
I know that must sound strange,
but I beg you to hear me out...
On that fateful day
when you first touched me,
I should've known my days
as an atheist were over.
Because looking back,
divine is the only way
I could describe that encounter.
Sure, you came to me via car
and not the clouds, but I swear
you floated all the same.
With a style and grace
that I have come to miss.
And I'll never forget
the way you looked up at me;
it was as if you were seeing me
for the very first time.
And it made me feel reborn.
Though I existed before that day,
in the peripheries of your life,
you somehow created a new man
that belonged only to you.
And while I don't know if you
were made from my rib or not,
I do know that by my side
was where you belonged.
Yet sadly, I now spend my days forsaken.
Wandering the desert,
where doubts have become dunes,
and you are nowhere to be found.
I wonder, is this my penance
for placing you on a pedestal?
Or is this the cost of loving you
more than our Creator?

THE HAMMER

Some days, darling, I treat
our memories like accomplishments.
As if they were awards,
displayed proudly upon
the shelves within my mind.
Yet on lonely nights like this,
I have a foolish tendency to
treat them like old movies.
Things to be dusted off and projected,
So they can be relived behind my eyes.
Truth be told,
that's the only way I see you nowadays.
The only way that I know you're still alive.
For they are my last bit of proof
that you truly existed;
and weren't just some figment
of my cruel imagination.
And that's why I can't help
but wish to take a hammer
to my memories tonight.
Because reaching out to you
in the present is pointless.
Your silence only leaves me feeling hollow.
And looking back on you,
and the things that we used to do,
that only makes me ache.
I'm fucking tired of feeling like
my best days in love are behind me.
And I'm tired of pretending that
your best love was only mine to feel;
and not the ones who came after me.
You were the best thing the old me
could've ever hoped to have, baby.
The sovereign I'm becoming, though?
Won't even remember your name,
once this hammer stops ringing.

CLYDE HURLSTON

THE NATURAL ORDER OF THINGS

In my eyes, she is the moon,
and I am her tide.
I spend my days churning in solitude,
just waiting for her arrival.
But now the natural order of things
are out of balance,
and I don't know what I can do to fix it.
You see? My moon
had been quiet as of late;
and when she returned
what she found upset her.
There was an anger in my waves,
and it showed in the written marks
they left behind.
And unfortunately,
she mistook my turbulence
toward a member of the world
as an affront towards her.
So she has turned away from me,
and I am lost without her light.
I am filled with shame,
knowing that I have
pained her in some way.
How can I survive knowing
the star of my dreams
believes me to be a nightmare?
I'm not sure. I just know
that I'll stay here churning,
and hoping for her forgiveness.
For there is no other that moves me
but her; and I miss her terribly.

MADE WHORES TO TIME

I refuse to believe this is natural...
Looking at all of us now,
I wonder how our ancestors would feel
seeing us all sitting in pitiful processions;
in our rolling soul coffins
made of plastic and metal,
as they regurgitate fumes into the air.
I wonder if those who kept time by the stars,
would surely laugh at us
for being submissive to that which
has but two small hands and a face.
I wonder if they would curse our names
once they learned the way we forsake
that which causes us to feel alive;
in exchange for promissory notes
and coins all in order to survive.
They would say we were
made whores to time...
Giving away our days by the hour
Giving away our sovereignty
and the spark of our divine power.
For trinkets that will become obsolete,
long before they are paid for.
And long after the interest has waned.

CLYDE HURLSTON

"SEDUCTION OF OUR SECONDS" ART BY MITCH GREEN

LOVE YOUR ENEMIES

I was told that a man said,
"no weapon formed
against you shall prosper."
And there were days when I believed him.
But when I look at my life today,
I must admit, I'm not so sure anymore.
For my doubts constantly assemble
and fortify their position in my mind.
Despite my attempts at denial,
anguish still hides within
the Trojan horse shaped like my words.
And an acidic hatred
invaded my heart many moons ago.
So I called out to the man and asked,
"What am I to do?
How can I win a war without end?"
And it was then that he whispered,
answering ever so clearly,
"You must love your enemies, my son.
The one in the mirror most of all."

CLYDE HURLSTON

CLIMB HIGHER

After all of this time,
I believe I have found
my place in this universe:
I am to be the stepping stone.
The springboard from which she,
and those like her,
have gone on to find
where they were meant to be.
I am the first rung
on the ladder made for angels.
I am merely there to aid the passage.
For I am a kind soul
with sympathetic ears.
With broad shoulders that are
both able and willing to
catch their tears or hold their worlds
for as long as they would need it.
But there always comes a time
when they tire of what is.
And they yearn for what can be.
So, they leave;
onward and upward.
Yet, while I lie here,
everything in my mind
wants me to hate her.
Though it seems my heart
just won't let me.
So all I will say to her now is
climb higher, my love.
May you find what you're looking for;
and may it be nothing like me.

MISTAKEN BELIEFS

Most people mistakenly believe
that growth only occurs beneath the sun.
And while the light is essential
to body, mind, and soul;
I am here to tell you that
it is not the all within The All.
The universe demands balance.
And that is why growth
also happens in the darkness.
Whether it is in the womb,
or beneath the moon,
we can still reach the places
the gods wish us to be.
Do you understand, dear friend?
Darkness is not our enemy.
No, it is simply tinder for your Light.

CLYDE HURLSTON

THE EMBERS OF MY SOUL

Though it still beats, I fear my heart
has been weighed against the feather;
and it is clear that I
have been found wanting.
For I believe that Ma'at would not
even turn her gaze upon me,
after what I have done.
And as surely as man
was said to be made from dust,
I have made excuses
out of circumstances.
Foolishly forgetting that
sometimes a kiss
becomes a prerequisite
for the spear
in the side of righteousness;
I must remember that
I am not the Savior,
nor am I the repentant thief.
I am simply an
easily-distracted student.
Trying in vain to follow
the footsteps of the masters
who have gone before him.
For the Ladder leads not to the temple,
and the Seven are far from unsealed.
And as a matter of fact,
who am I to even believe that
I deserve such Grace?
I don't know that I do.
And that is why I do my best
to smear this
bloody heart across the page.
Too many believe it to be
a decoration upon my sleeve,
and they fail to see it as a beacon.
So just in case I will never again

know the Light, I will choose
to leave the embers of my soul
behind for you. Here, still shining
and smoldering between the lines.
Please take care of them.

CLYDE HURLSTON

ECHOES & REFLECTIONS

Echoes and reflections,
have their games they like to play.
Seeking the potential for remembrance,
they'll invade throughout the day.
But I'm still learning to look away,
whilst preserving
the progress that I've made.
For I know the trees
we've labeled memories,
provide a little more than shade.
And I have been down that lonely road,
far too often it would seem.
Which abandoned
coherent thoughts to slumber,
while the reveries learned to scream.
Knowing I was strung out and captivated,
on a love that wouldn't last.
But now I dance amongst remains,
beneath the strata of her past.
I wonder can she visualize discomfort,
as I lie amidst the bones?
Having final visions of castle fires,
and the ash of empty thrones.

ROOM TO BREATHE

"It's time to move on," they say.
Time to stop worrying about the people
who don't even care that we're alive.
Time for the broken to pick up their pieces
and get on with their lives.
Well I think it's time to for us to wonder,
who the fuck asked you for your opinion?
I'll tell you… None of us.
Who the fuck are you
to tell another soul
when their wounds should be closed?
Were you even there
when the bleeding began?
Did you ever once fashion a tourniquet
to help the bleeding stop?
No? Well then, fuck you
and your judgments.
We all know that time heals all wounds;
but healing isn't done
in accordance with the second hand.
So how about you saved
your goddamn breath,
and give other souls the room to breathe?
Because that would easily be
the best thing you've ever done in life.

CLYDE HURLSTON

RISE

My friend,
I once commanded her to Pay Homage...
And I bid myself to Become Royal.
Yet for all intents and purposes,
neither of us have listened.
Truth be told,
I never really expected her to listen;
since taking orders was never her style.
It was one of the many things
I loved about her.
But I did always hope that
I would have listened;
so that in the process,
I could discover some things
I actually loved about myself.
Sadly, complacence has
fit me like a glove;
and in this tower,
my body has become a prison
shaped much like a comfort zone.
So it has been both a fear of failure
and a self-destructive train of thought
that keep me tethered to this place.
Reminding me that I have forgotten
the cardinal rule of change;
there is no such thing as trying.
One must find the courage,
the conviction, and the strength of will
to simply get it done.
For nothing worth having
comes without sacrifice.
Learn this, and then you can rise.

GREEK FIRE

For decades,
I searched high and low for you.
Then, seemingly out of nowhere,
you found me and resurrected
my soul with a kiss.
And it was your touch that made a man
that longed for death,
determined to squeeze every drop
of life from the coming days.
I fell for you far faster than I wanted to;
and so I could do nothing else
but write you into immortality.
Hoping to prove to you
that my love was Greek fire;
a dangerous, eternal force.
The flames danced proudly for you,
as I happily burned alive
in the hopes of keeping you warm
in this cold world.
But nowadays the burning
continues in vain,
as my dreams of reunion turn to ash.
In your heart,
a substitution has been made;
and what once burned high enough
for the gods to see,
has now become proof
of the fool I've made myself out to be.

CLYDE HURLSTON

WINDOWS

If eyes are the windows to the soul,
then the pains reflected
in these panes must be profound.
And make no mistake,
these particular windows
have seen their share of rainy days
since you've been gone;
but I don't even bother hiding from,
or planning for the
weather anymore, darling.
Because there's nothing that
the darkened clouds could gift me,
that your absence
hasn't already wrought.
So here I am,
screaming at the clouds
to do their worst;
let them rain on me
without warning, I say.
For these stinging drops on my skin
shall be the closest I'll ever get
to your touch again.
May the gods use them to
wash away your memory
and fill the hole you left behind.
Maybe then I'll know peace.

POUND OF FLESH

Even with everything
I've learned as of late,
I can't help but to feel like a fool.
As I struggle to bring balance to a mind,
I'm forced to have my heart
torn out of me on a daily basis.
And I can't help but feel
that there is no plan in all of this.
No grand design unfolding in real time;
and no purpose for the suffering we endure.
Sure, some will tell me
this is the will of their god;
and some will tell me to keep the faith.
Yet, for me, faith is but
a dressing upon the wound;
the blood still flows beneath it.
All the while, coaxing us to believe
that martyrdom makes us special;
when it doesn't.
Karma seems to take
its pound of flesh by the minute;
and soon there will be nothing left of us.
I'm just tired of having
the ones I love wish for death.
When I know good and goddamn well
I'm running out of reasons,
to convince them to
treasure each and every breath.
And I fear they're no longer listening.

CLYDE HURLSTON

LACED WITH HURT

I've watched as many tears were shed,
and a soul cried out in pain.
As the darkness sought to drown the night,
then came pouring down like rain.
And as this soul professed exhaustion,
my rage caused this chest to swell.
For I'd rather tear the fucking stars in half,
than to watch him live within this hell.
And where are the gods in all of this,
what parts will they decide to play?
Must I summon up the morning star,
and give my precious soul away?
Whilst knowing any deal I've signed in blood,
can never be undone.
But what choice is there left for us to take,
when our suffering's just begun?
Sure, I know there are many things we've yet to learn,
in these lessons laced with hurt.
Still our knees have kissed the Earth so many times,
they've now been stained with dirt.
So forgive me if my brittle faith,
begins to crumble down beneath the weight.
I just pray the light will find its way,
before its arrival is too late.

IF THERE BE SUCH A THING

At the risk of embarrassing myself,
I said exactly what
I had been meaning to say.
Where concrete walls
once stood tall and proud,
I could feel the break
as the dam was giving way.
Which caused the words to burst forth,
like a river unrestrained;
allowing me to finally tell her how I felt.
Since she went away.
And now I had done so
without hyperbole,
without placing the words
beneath the comforts of a veil.
This time I wrote, and she read.
But after the roar of
the rapids died down,
all that was left was the silence.
The very silence which
watered my perspective
and forced something else to grow here.
For the trees once green with envy,
had to fall and never make a sound.
Just as I too had fallen on my face,
having fast become
reacquainted with the ground.
There was nothing left
to be said, it seems.
Replies and their echoes
would only live in
the silver lining of my dreams.
Tucked gently beneath
the thought of "someday,
I'll be viewed as royalty again."
Maybe in the next life,
if there be such a thing.
Who am I to say?

CLYDE HURLSTON

WHERE THE ARROW LANDS

By the unseen hands,
the arrow is held in place
as the string of the bow is drawn back.
As we ourselves are pulled into the light,
the arrow is released.
Though it has passed the point of no return,
it is unaware that we shall grow
to bear witness of its flight.
Eventually, we become painfully aware
of its trajectory; and by "chance",
we wade into what we believe to be its waters.
And within those currents,
all we truly discover is humility.
For we are taught a harsh lesson
in our own insignificance.
Like the curious children we were,
we find that our perceptions allow us
to flail our arms within the waters.
Our ego, our collective hubris
are but anchors chained and bound
to feet that wish to kick.
But there is no fighting the stream.
Whether we swim,
whether we stay stagnant and drown,
or whether we even try
going against the tide, it matters not;
the waters shall run regardless.
It is only when our arms no longer flail,
and our lights begin to dim,
that we finally discover
just where the arrow lands.
And yet a few of us have learned,
that it never did at all.

RESUME TILLING

In my time mourning
the loss of her love,
I realized that I had
fallen off the path.
The journey I was on
required the bulk of my focus.
There wasn't time for me
to bleed out upon the pages,
hoping she would see them and return;
for I had wonders to discover.
Now that the veil was being
pulled off of the lines written so long ago,
I was reminded by great teachers
of exactly where the kingdom lies.
And that it isn't heartbreak
that will help free us
from our collective bondage;
but rather, it is truth.
Truth is the only thing
that can save us from this hell
that we endure,
along with living in
accordance with The Seven.
So while the void she left remains,
I must rebuild myself from within.
Then and only then
may I enter the temple
built with no hands;
and relight the torch
using the fire from the gods.
Lighting the way
for those still too blind to see.
Today, I have resumed my tilling;
so that seeds sown may still grow.

CLYDE HURLSTON

A FOG INSIDE THE MIND

It is only when the fog
inside the mind dissipates,
that man can begin to see clearly.
For the rising of tensions,
no matter the level of danger,
is but foreplay to the baser natures of man.
You see, it is the release
that an orgasm brings,
that speaks to the mage within him.
But it is the silence
in the aftermath of war,
that finally calms the beast within him.
It is only in those respective quiets,
that he is given insight
into what he has done.
And I can only hope that a man
is forever greeted by the sight
of the lover he has pleased,
and not the spent shells
and scarred remains of the souls
he has sent to the great beyond.
Because no matter who
is labeled the victor,
when diplomacy gives way to violence,
there is no one that ever wins.
For ghosts are only known
to haunt the living,
and I would much prefer the pleasure
I receive from giving.
May the light of the gods
forever keep the beast in me at bay.
Since the last thing I'd ever want to do,
is take the life of another soul away.
Unless it was to save those
I have come to love.
So I guess it is how a wise man once said:
"Sometimes you have to be a lion,
in order to be the lamb you really are."

SEEING IS BELIEVING

It's been said that seeing is believing;
and by the upward gazing among us,
it's said that it's better
to believe without having seen.
For they claim that is where
the true power lies.
Yet I myself, have never known
the taste of power.
Sure, I have used physical force
in my day to day labors;
and I have felt the pull of my heart
when it was given to a woman
who once loved me.
Yet, this power they speak of
with reverence, still eludes me.
And when the proliferation of questions
rear their ugly heads,
they reach for their semantics
as if they were sidearms.
Biases are then wielded
without concern for bystanders.
Unaware, that their actions
prove nothing more than my Tower
being a part of the one
they built so long ago.
They view my vantage as devoid,
and I view theirs as convenient.
If only they would look beyond the veil
as I am trying to do...
Only then would they find the place
where a man once wrestled an angel.
For I have yet to find one
in the sky or upon the pedestals
I once built for them.

CLYDE HURLSTON

SATISFY YOURSELF

They all say the same thing,
in a myriad of ways;
it's just the proverbial
window dressing that's different.
Don't be fooled by
their supposed intentions
or their physical attributes.
Beneath all of the
department store veneer,
beneath the strength found
in quotes and self-discovered divinity,
the same patterns are at work.
And upon thorough examination
of the tapestry,
you will not find loyalty amidst the coding.
Your best bet is to take
what is given willingly
and move on to the next one.
For building pedestals
will earn you only apathy,
and love is just a pretty name
we give to graves for the living.
Don't waste your time,
don't waste any second
of your precious life;
satisfy your own urges.

PLANTING TREES

Why are they surprised
that a generation raised on lies
is now starving for the truth?
How could they be shocked
that we've reached a point,
where there is little to us
that's beyond contestation?
From the very existence of God
to the perceived roundness of the Earth,
it seems nothing is certain to us anymore.
We've just learned to
expect betrayal and dishonesty.
To prepare ourselves for the worst,
whilst simultaneously hoping for the best.
Yet, it is on days like these,
that I find myself without hope.
For very few know the pain
of lying awake amongst the slumbering.
The sadness that comes when
enlightenment blossoms into alienation.
The tragedy of learning that
even the closest of lovers exist
on the wrong side of temporality.
This world is not what it appears to be,
and its people are simply prone
to become better liars; myself included.
So why do we risk even
getting out of bed in the morning?
It is because a wise man
suggested we plant trees,
knowing we will never sit in their shade.
And I believe that he was right.

CLYDE HURLSTON

THE BULL LEADS TO BEAR

Tell me, have you heard the story, friend?
About the one who lost it all?
No, this isn't a tale that warns of risk,
or pride coming before the fall.
No, this is about the one
who played the odds,
knowing that life was far from fair.
Still, optimism was trading high,
until the market was proven bear.
Now so many claim to see potential,
despite their failures to invest.
And commodities maintain their worth,
when they remain closer to the chest.
But if a soul is trading publicly,
their best bet is denial.
Then it's easier to withhold the truth,
if the case ever goes to trial.
Still they offer up encouragement,
and suggest we stay the course.
Regurgitating all clichés,
until their collective voice was hoarse.
Yet their money is seldom ever found,
in the place from which they speak.
Instead they look at those
who have given up,
as true examples of the weak.
My, how easy that is for them to say...

AS OLD AS TIME

I bid you to laugh and
worry not, my brother.
Smile and do not fret, my sister.
For the light still lives within us all.
Even on the days that
draw envy from the night,
I assure you, it lives.
You must remember this always.
For when the precious seconds
are crushed beneath the weight
of the bleakest hours,
the dawn still comes in time.
And I have learned that
it is only when we are left without choice,
that our true selves are oft revealed.
While conversely,
it's in our moments of weakness,
that our truths are buried or concealed.
Yet, despite our desires,
we learn that the truth will have its day.
Whether we learn this through
repetition or discovery, it matters not.
The truth comes to those who seek it;
those who deny it are left
beneath the tumultuous waves
of their own hubris.
To be broken against
the stones as old as time.

CLYDE HURLSTON

PUZZLE PIECES

I believe there is something wrong with me;
that I must be damaged
in some kind of obvious way.
But it seems that
with the more people I meet,
we're all broken in some form or fashion.
Reality has taken its toll on all of us, I fear.
Yet, here we all are, walking puzzle pieces.
Looking desperately to find
the other piece that will fit best beside us.
And sadly, most of us are still searching.
But if you were to ask me why,
I'd say it's because these days,
the one whose hands made me feel whole
now lays them upon another.
And since then,
when the days get dark enough,
even the new moon forsakes the ocean.
So what am I to do?
How does one dull the jagged edge
that stops others from getting close?
I honestly don't know.
But I guess with enough time,
everything dulls; not just the senses.
I just never thought her love would...

THE LAST STAND

Though I'm not allowed inside the lodge,
on some nights,
I have considered myself a builder.
And that is because
throughout my young life,
that I have built pedestals
to hold the undeserving.
And more recently,
during the depths of my loneliest nights,
I have erected monoliths
in the name of moons that shine
but no longer dance.
Such is the fate of a misguided prophet.
Who knew that by speaking
my truths without resistance,
that I would manifest
more of the same into existence?
Certainly not I, my friend.
Yet, now that I am fully aware
of the power of words,
I feel them losing their grip
over the man who once longed
to capture them for the sake of eternity.
For he knows the darkness
is looming upon the horizon;
and he is preparing to
make his last stand.
So whatever happens
from this point on,
know that I wish you all the best.
Now and forever.

CLYDE HURLSTON

WHEN GIANTS WALKED THE EARTH

Unsure of his every step,
he lumbered
throughout his adolescence.
Feeling as if he was
a giant among dwarves
or a whale amongst fish,
he often feared to move.
For around him, the weaker chairs
and benches were in danger
and unsuspecting bed frames
weren't safe either.
Each item broken overwhelmed him
with shame and sent him
further into himself.
His voice never growing
to mirror the cannons he heard
on the glowing screens;
but rather it was often strained
when he was forced
by circumstance to speak.
Eventually he made a selfish decision
and compounded it
by not listening to his instincts.
In doing so, he would come to learn
that he failed his greatest friend.
An act from which the seeds of depression
and self-loathing would find
fertile soil in which to take root.
Creating endless darkened trees
in his mind, through which he would
never see the forest.
The boy then grew to become
the ugly beast who deserved
this tower he lives in;
despite what anyone else may tell you.

SHOULDERS OF EVEREST

I don't remember exactly
how it happened, but it did.
I retreated into the shell I created for myself.
The walls I had erected, felt like they stood
shoulder to shoulder with Everest.
Each wall had a name.
Pain, despair, stress, and loneliness.
And I realized that my bitterness
built a lid they labeled "anger."
So, in time, this life became a tomb,
in which I slowly buried myself alive.
For years, I felt unwanted and alone.
Breathing felt like a punishment
I was forced to endure.
But that all changed.
I can't tell you how,
because that must remain a secret.
A truth known to no one but me.
But the shell has begun to crack.
I can feel the sun
starting to make its way inside.
And I'm sad to say that it's been
a very long time since I felt the light.
And yeah, I'll admit,
it does burn a little at first.
But now, it's starting to feel
a little more bearable in here.
Who knows, maybe with a little more light,
a lot of love, and just a bit of luck,
confidence can begin to grow again.
And I can be the first king
to emerge from the tomb alive.
Because, after years of feeling
like the living dead,
I can say with all of my heart,
that these days I'm dying to live.

CLYDE HURLSTON

HE STILL LIVES

To the man that simply exists,
death is but a relief.
To the man that burns with life,
death is an enemy.
One to be fought
with every drop of sweat and
every ounce of vigor that one possesses.
For he knows death is waiting in the wings.
Slowly chipping away
at the time he has left.
So that is why he cannot afford
to waste his days.
For there is far too much left to do.
Too much left to see.
Too many things that he has yet to be.
And that is why he yearns to create
something worth leaving behind.
So that when death finally
comes for him, he can laugh.
Knowing that even as he passes
beyond the veil... he still lives.

WHEN THE RIVERS RUN DRY

Someone once said I was prolific;
given the way that words
flowed freely from my fabled reservoir.
Yet these days,
a dam has been erected
around this proverbial Black Sea.
This ink-filled ocean of emotions.
Occasionally, a piece may leak out
for old time's sake;
but for the most part,
the words no longer flow
with any regularity.
Some say it is because
I am in need of a break.
Others claim it is
because I lack a muse.
Yet, if the truth be told,
I actually lack desire.
I don't want to do this.
I don't want to write anymore.
I want to finish my next collection
and be done with this.
One last nail in the coffin of a dream.
Then there'll be no need for muses
or enduring their betrayals.
There'll be no need
for constant seppuku upon the page;
leaving my entrails between the lines
to be critiqued by those I do not know.
There will simply be the one thing
that was always loyal to me: Silence.
The true love of my life.
And I am sorry if this upsets you all;
but my soul is tired
and my eyes are cried out.
Time to move on.

CLYDE HURLSTON

IT'S TIME

I can feel the end drawing closer...
So that is why, I'm tidying up
the proverbial desk, just a little bit.
And I thought for sure that this
would feel less like
the closing of a chapter,
and more like losing a part of myself...
But it turns out,
I don't feel anything at all.
Even the usual emptiness is gone.
And while I should feel grateful, I don't.
This has been too long overdue.
So I continue putting away
the parts of me that I've exposed for too long.
It's time this heart came off my sleeve,
and was put back into my vacant chest;
never to be seen again.
It's time I put the cap back on my inkwell,
and placed my quill back into its case.
And lastly, it's time I carefully put away
the blank sheets of paper I have left;
and I thank them for helping to save my life.
Then I apologize,
because I have no plans
to ever see them again.
But as I said before: it's time.

THE LITTLE BOOK

Today I felt the sharpest pain,
radiating outward from my chest.
The source was to me, a mystery,
So its origin was greeted with a guess.
But then the cause would find my eyes,
and I wish I had never asked.
And as I then, began to bleed
I realized I had to find some paper fast.
For today I was forced to watch,
the death of my longest waking dream.
Proving that things once said aloud,
are never ever what they seem.
No, some times they are simply said,
to cruelly tease the ones that hear.
And others use their words to provoke
and fill the listener with fear.
Worse yet, they could inspire hope
to exist despite the circumstance.
By claiming stars that were never crossed
could somehow find a way to dance.
But that, dear friends, was another lie
to compound the many told
Leaving deleted pictures and memories
as the only things to hold.
And now the little book I once compiled
as both proof and testament to love
Must be thrown into the flames
I pray every moth will rise above.
For they're not the worth the pain endured
no matter what each page may have said.
I just wish I could somehow do the same
to the their place inside my head.

CLYDE HURLSTON

A LIFE LIVED IN PRINT

When you live your life upon the page,
betrayal comes in many forms.
A crease here, a tear there.
Maybe a voice was even
silenced by a bookmark;
the possibilities are myriad.
Still, few sting worse than selective vision.
And were I a lesser man,
I would still allow my lens
to be tainted by expectations.
But I have since learned
the error in those ways.
For I find that souls do
what they must to survive in the moment;
knowing justifications can always
be tailored at a later time.
As if planted seeds don't grow in darkness...
as if tears don't feel like rain
to the unsuspecting soil.
No matter, dear reader...
when all is said and done,
blood and ink are one and the same.
The wells that produced them
just come in different shapes.
And it seems that most
do not find the one offered to their liking.

HARVEST DARKNESS

If you're planting shadows to
harvest darkness,
You will disappoint the sun.
And legs grow weary on ground unsteady,
and so they seldom run.
Still ungodly notions spring to some minds,
once our silhouettes are seen.
While shores erode beneath the weight of,
each new wave upon the scene.
And i wish i had the long sought answers,
that drew you to this page.
But I'm afraid that I'm not a genius,
and all the world's a stage.
All you will find offered here, my dear
is the truth expressed in ink.
Which I hope will penetrate your mind,
while we are still allowed to think.
But the truth so rarely brings us riches,
still, the gods demand we take a stand.
Before the shadows choose to pull our number,
and place the weapon in our weaker hand.

CLYDE HURLSTON

HOW CAN IT BE SAID OF ME?

Cowardice and insecurity
bar me from the stage.
But when my dripping pen
finally feels the waiting page.
I am alive - and able to be. Truly me.
For I am free. I am free. I am free.
Clumsiness and two left feet,
make my movements awkward; often incomplete.
But the quill glides so effortless,
revealing sentiments often bittersweet.
Still, I am alive and
I am free. I am free. I am free.
Blank lines will mirror wolves,
howling loud for resplendent moons.
While enticing ink will coax virgin butterflies,
to wake and transcend cocoons.
For they are like me - alive...
And we are free. We are free. We are free.
As imagined fingertips get drunk on skin,
and Eden's gates part to take me in.
I can think of no greater sacrament,
than manifesting thought and written sin.
O Heaven of mine, I am alive inside of you.
And I am free. I am free. I am free.
Rivers flow with steady red,
as plumes of smoke and ash rise to choke the air.
Flashing screens transmit the scenes,
but atop the hill they are lacking care.
And I will now forsake the booth, since I can see...
They are not free. They are not free. They are not free.
God save us all, they are not free.
So how can the opposite be said of me?

DODGING ARROWS

Would you look at us?
And I mean, really look at us.
How the gods must laugh at us all.
Through their eyes,
we must look like children.
Squabbling amongst ourselves over toys,
whilst simultaneously destroying Eden.
All the while looking upward
and never inward.
All the while, living out of fear.
Spending our precious days dodging arrows.
Whether they be from Cupid's quiver
or the arrow we imagine
leaving the fingers of Chronos;
we dodge them all the same.
Doing anything possible
to avoid being struck by either
of their respective heads,
out of fear of losing our own.
But such things are beyond our control.
We are but slaves to entropy.
So knowing this,
we mustn't allow our hearts
to fall prey to atrophy.
For we will never know
how many beats we have left.
So I beg you,
make each one of them count.
Let those beats echo
within your chest like war drums.
And may your life be filled
with only that which moves you deeply...
Just like the arrows.

CLYDE HURLSTON

OUR LAST DAYS

Some will say that life
is nothing more than a series of events.
An interlinked chain of moments
and memories remembered fondly.
But of course, these recollections
will be well-seasoned with mistakes;
And bear the unmistakably
permanent fingerprints
of triumph and tragedy.
Still, when all is said and done,
and our last days are lived,
our skin will display the lines
of the story that time has written.
Leaving our bones behind,
like a whispered secret inside the Earth.
Eventually, reuniting ashes with the dust.
And proving that the grains inside the glass
will show us no mercy;
Despite them being neither friend nor foe.
But I still find myself choosing to pray
that whomever reads this
will find a way to make
every single word of their story count.

WHEN THE ANGELS SING

When the time was right, the gods
finally allowed the parting of the gates.
And like the proverbial babe lost in the woods,
he slowly made his way into the Holy Garden.
Reticent; but eager to experience
paradise for himself.
But still, here he was...
in the earthly Heaven known as Eden.
Naturally, his breath was taken from him.
A fitting penance; seeing as
such splendor requires adjustment.
For this is not a place that intends
to host those souls whom
are unable to compose themselves.
Patience and endurance
would certainly be requisite here;
for there are countless wonders
that require one's attention.
With the grace of her outstretched hand,
the horned angel would
guide him proudly.
Placing him exactly where
she required him the most.
Thankfully for all, it was a location
he was well-equipped to reach.
So, it wasn't long before she instructed him
to remain where he was,
and to continue without stopping.
And he knew exactly what she meant;
so her wish was his command.
Feeling confident, he then made one of his own:
"Do not close your eyes, my love.
Let me see where you go,
when your eyes roll back
and the angels begin to sing."
And it was there,
that they would both find God.
For it is said where His name is spoken,
He is there. So I would imagine,
He is there when it is screamed as well.

CLYDE HURLSTON

STAR MAPS

Tell me the truth, dear reader...
Please let me know that
this ink is not spilled in vain.
For I have done my very best,
to mine this mind of mine,
and find everything
of value within it.
Then I have taken the treasures found,
and sown them between these lines.
Watering them all
with a potent potion
of blood, sweat, and tears.
Foolishly hoping they will manifest
into star maps before your very eyes;
allowing you all to make sense of
the constellations I suppress within myself.
Not out of fear they will shine, mind you.
But out of concern that they will draw
vultures instead of moths.
For I have never known
the admiration of souls.
I have simply existed in a myriad of rooms
where I have gone unseen.
And I say these somber things
not out of a desire for sympathy,
but rather to express my gratitude.
Seeing as that fresh ink on your hands,
tells me that these carefully laid treasures
have great value, after all.

DIGGING FOR SUNLIGHT (DEAR PAGE)

Hello again, Dear Page...
It's that time again.
I'm here with another secret
to share with you.
I've told you so many over the years.
It's been hard to keep track of them all.
But this one,
I'm surprised you haven't figured out already.
And that secret is,
is that I have often imagined myself in Hell...
I'm sure that sounds
strange on the surface;
but I swear to you dear,
that it is the truth.
Because even though
I am grateful to be alive,
I understand the situation
I now find myself in.
And if I'm being as honest
as I have been known to be,
I don't know if I have the strength
to dig myself out of here.
Up and out of this hole,
and up and out of this tomb of flesh,
I have buried myself within.
You see, Dear Page,
I've spent so long
taking care of every one else,
that I have allowed myself
to go to waste.
And mind you, that's not because
of the love I gave to others;
but rather, the lack of love
I have always had for myself.
I've long since believed that I deserved
to remain the way that I am.
To punish myself
for conscious mistakes I made,
when I was but a child.
Even though I know better as a man.

And that is why I imagine myself in Hell.
It's where people like me
are supposed to go for not believing.
It's where people like me
are supposed to go for what I've done.
And it's where people like me,
currently find ourselves living.
Not many souls live the life of the unchosen.
They don't know what it's like,
to not exist in a crowded room.
They don't know what it's like,
to never be selected for anything.
Shit, they don't even know what it's like,
to feel so painfully alone
in a room full of friends and family.
But such is life, Dear Page...
They will never understand me
the way that you do.
They will only offer hollow advice,
or regale me with the tales
of the successes of others.
And the saddest part of all,
will be that I know they are right...
but when are you this far down,
and some days it hurts
to even fucking breathe...
Then it's hard to find the strength
to raise your arms,
those arms that are tired
from treading dirt like water...
Yeah, it's hard to find
the strength to raise them
over your head
full of discouraging voices,
and finally start digging for sunlight.

A BEAUTIFUL DOOM

AND SO WE'VE REACHED THE END

"I do not fear death.
I had been dead for billions and billions of years
before I was born, and had not suffered
the slightest inconvenience from it."

- Mark Twain

"For what is it to die
but to stand naked in the wind
and to melt into the sun?
And when the earth shall claim your limbs,
then shall you truly dance."

- Kahlil Gibran

"The life you have left is a gift.
Cherish it.
Enjoy it now, to the fullest.
Do what matters, now."

- Leo Babauta

CLYDE HURLSTON

"Death smiles at us all,
all a man can do is smile back."

- Marcus Aurelius

"If a man hasn't discovered something
that he will die for, he isn't fit to live."

- Dr. Martin Luther King, Jr.

"What do we say to the Lord of Death? 'Not today.' "

- George R. R. Martin

A BEAUTIFUL DOOM

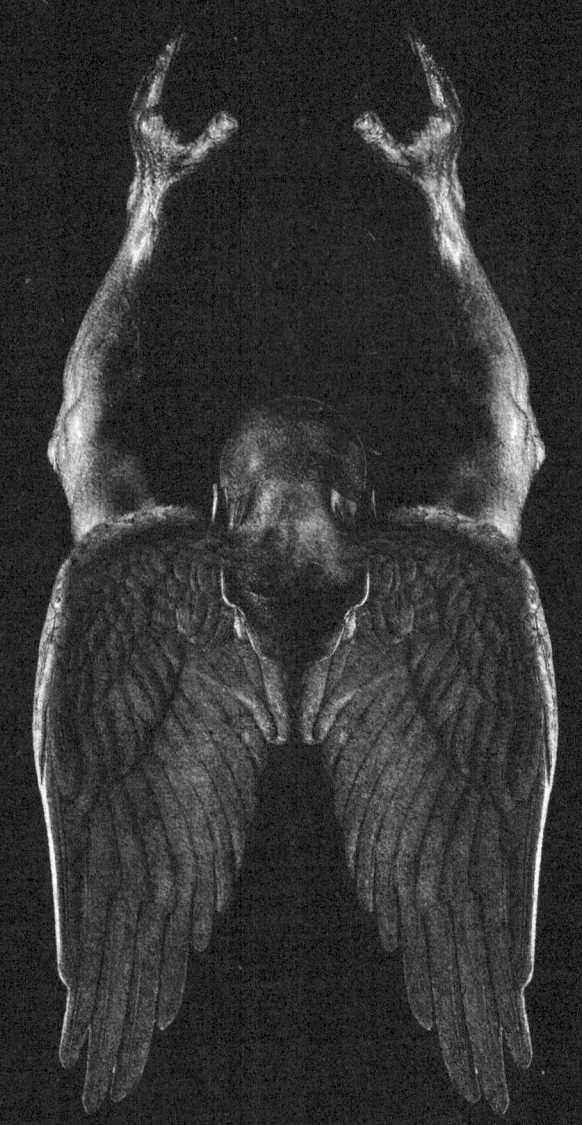

"WHY ANGELS HAVE WINGS" ART BY MITCH GREEN

CLYDE HURLSTON

"We see a hearse; we think sorrow.
We see a grave; we think despair.
We hear of a death; we think of a loss.
Not so in heaven.
When heaven sees a breathless body,
it sees the vacated cocoon & the liberated butterfly."

- Max Lucado

Reflections Of Janus recommends these other books from Clyde R. Hurlston

www.ingramcontent.com/pod-product-compliance
Lightning Source LLC
Chambersburg PA
CBHW040639100526
44585CB00039B/2819